Poker Nights

Poker Nights

Rules, Strategies, & Tips for the Home Player

Scott Tharler

BARRON'S

First edition for the United States and Canada published by
Barron's Educational Series, Inc., 2004 and reprinted 2005.

Produced by PRC Publishing
The Chrysalis Building
Bramley Road, London W10 6SP

An imprint of **Chrysalis** Books Group plc

© 2004 PRC Publishing

All inquiries should be addressed to:
Barron's Educational Series, Inc.
250 Wireless Boulevard
Hauppauge, NY 11788
http://www.barronseduc.com

International Standard Book No. 0 7641 2888 4

Library of Congress Catalog Card No. 2003114847

Printed in China

9 8 7 6 5 4 3 2

Dedication

To my dad and his poker buddies of the last 35 years:
Ed Aaronson, Jerry Finkel, Denis Friedman, Royce Ginn,
Bill Gratz, Jules Gordon, Dave Manalan, Nick
Mozzicato, Bruce Smith, Sandy Sanford, and Gerson
Stutman. Thanks for letting me sneak downstairs after
bedtime, listen to the banter, and peer over the table.
And decades later, for letting me play alongside the
big boys, when a trip back home happened to coin-
cide with one of those magical Thursday nights.

Contents

Acknowledgments

I am grateful for the love of my parents Elaine Lansky and Steven Tharler, sister Marni Tharler, and grandparents David and Sara Lansky and Stanley and Muriel Tharler.

Thanks for the camaraderie and inspiration of these players: David Isaac, Josh Weissman, JJ Wolf, Chuck Riedl, Gene Desrochers, Dave Coronella, Trevor Dellecave, Big Dave, Dan Dupont, Dave Crvelin, Neil Ishibashi, James Conway, Robert Funk, Phil DeGirolamo, Steve Meyerson, Adam Kowalczyk, Brian Heinen, and Keith Goldberg. And to the KDR brothers at JMU and Cincinnati, for those memorable all-night sessions.

Thanks to Jay Ehret, Dave Matson, Richard Lansky, Jennifer Wetter, Larry Hartung, Ashley Brooks, Susanna Speirs, and Nicholas Wong for their helpful suggestions.

I owe a special thanks to my aunt Vicki Lansky, uncle Bruce Lansky, and cousin Doug Lansky for their ongoing advice.

I am indebted to James Weingarten, Mike Fox, Wil Fox, Regie Belen, David Isaac, and Steven Tharler, for helping me through the tough times.

And last but not least, I appreciate the deal making of Martin Howard, the leadership of Frank Hopkinson, and the tireless efforts of Cheryl Thomas and everyone else at PRC who made this project possible.

Introduction

The standard "dealer's choice" format enjoyed by millions of home poker players implies an array of ways the cards could be dealt, the hands could be formed, and the winners could be determined, in addition to a range of rules that could be added to any game to "make it more interesting." Of course, simply knowing how to play and playing well are two different things. But by reading this book and then practicing, you could not only become a better-informed player, but also be...

1. **A more prepared player.** Able to understand most game situations right away.
2. **A more flexible player.** Able to adapt to any unfamiliar formats or features quicker.
3. **A more respected player.** Able to ask the right questions prior to playing. ("Can I buy an extra card with a 4 in the hole?" "Are the Queens themselves wild?" "Is there a buy in the end?")
4. **A more realistic player.** Able to ignore what may seem like small stakes (especially as compared to what the pros play with on television) in favor of smart, solid gameplay.
5. **A more competitive player.** Able to know what may win, thus surmise which hands (not) to pursue.
6. **A more social player.** Able to focus on enjoying the entertainment value of the evening more.
7. **A more skillful player.** Able to appreciate the subtle nuances that make poker special: How to recognize patterns, read people, react to situations, and make better strategic decisions—both at and away from the table!

How To Use This Book

This book neither requires nor teaches superior mathematical abilities. Home poker players don't necessarily need to know that they have a 1 in 23 chance of drawing two cards to an inside straight. They just need to know it ain't a good idea! In lieu of nonstop number-crunching, hone your instincts through vigilant play over time. During that time, you're sure to get more familiar with the all-important lingo of the game. In the meantime, if you ever see a strange term in the text that isn't immediately explained, check the glossary.

Although descriptions earlier in the book pave the way for what comes later, cross-references are provided throughout to make it easier for you to skip around. Along the way, you'll see aliases listed where a game is popularly known by more than one name. And conversely, where completely different games are known by the same name (namely with "Auction," "Black Mariah," "Murder," and "Pyramid"), numbers in parentheses follow to distinguish them, the ultimate goal being to quickly identify whatever the game is called and get right into playing!

Speaking of which, the "Playing" part of each game description is designed to be as concise as possible. While "Options & Variations" lists the most common mutations to discuss, make whatever modifications are necessary to fit each game into your group's style. Most of the other descriptions are self-explanatory. But what's likely to win in a particular game depends on the number of people playing, their skill level and understanding of the game, plus the randomness of what's dealt.

Finally, poker has traditionally been predominantly played by 25- to 65-year-old males in the United States. But it is currently enjoying a big boom, to the enjoyment of men and women of all ages in a growing number of places all over the world. So *Poker Nights* is definitely meant for anyone interested in the game!

Pre-Play

Unless Otherwise Stated...

For beginners not familiar with poker gameplay, the following fast primer:

Six or seven players are gathered. The host determines the first official dealer of the night by dealing face-up cards around the table. The player who gets the first Ace chooses/deals the first game. Those wishing to play toss an ante in the pot. After all the cards are shuffled, the player to the dealer's right may cut the deck. Each deal begins with the player to the dealer's left and continues one card at a time, face-down, clockwise. Each betting round starts with the player with the best hand showing (in an "open" game) or, if none of the players' hands is showing (a "closed" game), defaults to the player to the dealer's left.* That player may "check" (pass) or "bet." The bet continues clockwise.** Once a bet has been made, the next player can no longer check and must "call" (match the bet), "raise" (increase the bet), or fold (turn their cards face-down). Folded players are out of the action (receiving cards, betting, etc.)

You Bet!—Part I

How you bet is a huge part of poker—in some games, arguably more important than the actual cards you hold!

You can bet in one of four ways:

- *Check.* With a weak hand, it's a temporary stay of execution. (You'd welcome a free ride, but plan to fold if anyone bets anything substantial.) With a strong hand, it's a way of sizing up the competition. (You don't want to scare anyone away and do plan to call—or, if allowed, raise—the bet.) Either way, you strategically defer to the other players to set the pace that round.
- *Bet.* Because of your position relative to the dealer, the strength of your hand and/or the fact that everyone before you checked, you are first to place between the house minimum and maximum into the pot.
- *Call.* With no raises, it simply means matching the current bet in order to continue playing. If others have raised since your last bet within the same round, those must be factored. (See "You Bet—Part II" for specific examples.)
- *Raise.* Increasing the bet someone else made. In an attempt to either build the pot (if you have a strong hand) or get players to fold (if you're bluffing with a weak hand).

You Bet!—Part II

When sizing your bet or raise, consider the following:

- *Do you want players to call you?* If so, against conservative players you might otherwise scare away, a small to medium-sized bet (based on the house limits) makes sense.
- *Are you early or late to act?* If early, a big bet indicates a very good hand, since you know you could be raised and still don't mind making the investment (and presumably calling any later raises).
- *Has anyone else indicated strength?* If another player raised the bet last round, you may want to check this round. By "checking to the raiser," you take away their ability to raise your bet.
- *How did you act in the same situation last time?* As you'll see, there are often multiple possible tactics. A master bettor is self-aware and knows how to maximize his hands in a variety of situations.
- *How vulnerable are you?* If you have a hand that could improve to win (but has little chance without improving), bet the max earlier on. (Later on, players are less likely to fold.)
- *How much more will you have to bet to see the hand through?* In other words, don't just focus on the current bet. Plan ahead. Consider all the other bets and raises you might face if you stay in until it's clear whether you're the winner or not. If the idea of those multiple bets makes you nervous—or you don't think you could be the winner!—it's probably a good idea to fold and save your pennies for another hand.

for the rest of the hand and mustn't indicate anything about their hand. Once all the bets are called, the round is over. After the last round, the winner is the player with the best five-card hand.

To take the pressure off the player to the dealer's left, additional betting rounds can begin with another player one to the left.

**Good players wait for the action to get to them, to avoid being rude or giving away their intentions!*

You Bet!—Part III

Becoming more comfortable with the contextual rhythm of betting is an integral part of growing as a poker player. Disregarding the particular game and cards, let's study a typical betting round (read left to right):

Player 1	Player 2	Player 3	Player 4	Player 5	Player 6
"Check"	"25 cents"	"Call"	"Let's make it 50"	"Call"	"50 better"
"I call"	"I'm out"	"Too much"	"Bump 50 more"	"I fold"	"Call"
"Too rich for me"					

The first key to understanding the action is keeping track of the number and amount of raises after a bet is made. For instance, since Player 2 opened for 25 cents, Player 4 raised it 25 cents* and Player 6 re-raised it 50 cents, we know that Player 6 initially bet $1 (25 cents + 25 cents + 50 cents).

The next key is remembering your relative position to the action. Thus Player 1—who hadn't bet anything to that point—called by also betting $1. Players 2 and 3 folded. Player 4 put in $1 (50 cents for Player 6's raise and another 50 for his own re-raise). Player 5 folded. Player 6 still owed 50 cents from the last raise. And Player 1 folded.

The final key is knowing what it all amounts to. So how much money was contributed to the pot this round? If you said $5, you're probably ready to try it with actual chips, cards, and people!

*Player 4's sloppy 50-cent bet implies a 25-cent raise. But Player 5 might easily misinterpret it as the amount of a raise, not the total bet. On the other hand, it would've also been a no-no to have used the clichéd format, "I'll see your 25 [pause] and raise it 25." It's known as a "string bet" and isn't fair to the next player because they may be baited into prematurely acting (folding or going for their chips to make a bet) based on the call statement. Thus it's best when raising to simply state the amount of the raise.

Serving Stakes and Chips...

The assumed stakes are 25-cent antes with an initial $1 maximum bet/raise and an optional $2 max in the last betting round(s). Given these relatively low, fixed limits and three chip colors, it makes sense to assign chip values of 25 cents, 50 cents, and a dollar. Ideally, the preliminary "buy-in" (trade of cash for chips) might be $20, giving each player 20 quarter chips ($5), 20 half-dollars ($10), and five dollar chips ($5). All these amounts can obviously be scaled up/down based on the number of players and available chips. Whatever the stakes, the ante should be minimal. The max bet should make players think twice about staying in, especially when considering the number of betting rounds. And the buy-in should allow for enough chips to play several aggressive hands, but not exceed the cost of a cheap night out.

The Rules of the House...

Before a single chip or card hits the table, establish:

- Whether the ante will be done individually (25 cents by each player is assumed throughout, unless otherwise stated) or collectively ($2 by the dealer for everyone) — the latter of which avoids any confusion about missing antes at the start of each game.
- Whether players are allowed to "sandbag" (check and then later raise in the same betting round). It's a valid strategic move, but sometimes frowned upon in "friendly" games.
- If there's a standard three "bump" max (limiting the number of raises that are in any round of betting).
- If Aces are assumed to be both high and low or just high.* Especially important in games like "Screw Your Neighbor" (Section 12), "High-Low," and "Chicago" (both Section 2).
- The best Low hand (see the "Uninventing the Wheel" sidebar in Section 2).
- The accepted method of betting/declaring in split games (see the "Well, I Do Declare" sidebar in Section 2).

*Regardless, the rest of the cards rank: 2, 3, 4, 5, 6, 7, 8, 9, 10, Jack, Queen, King.

As displayed throughout the book, all poker games are subject to localizations. The host may add/enforce any other such house rule(s) or preferred variations as deemed acceptable.

It Takes All Types...

Once you know the games, the stakes, and the house rules, focus on whom you're playing against. Observe how your opponents bet, what they say, and how they react in various situations. Notice whether they seem to...

- Be quiet or talkative
- Bluff often or never raise
- Pay attention or always seem lost
- Play confidently or overthink every move
- Put an emphasis on mathematics or luck
- Play "tight" (conservative) or "loose" (wild, overly optimistic)
- Know every game or continually need the rules re-explained
- Quickly fold or always stay in—either stubornly or "just to be social"—no matter what the bet

And to whatever degree you're able to "read" (detect) these archetypical attributes in your adversaries, adjust your play. For example, don't raise the bet to try to get out someone who knows every game and always stays in. Conversely, when a typically conservative, probability-driven player raises your bet, fold! The flip side to all this is in how other players read you. Intermediate players vary their bet sizes (by situation) in order to be tougher to read. More advanced players carefully manipulate everything they say and do in order to build whatever façade they want rivals to believe! The bottom line is that reputations are crucial. So monitor yourself and others to the best of your abilities while still keeping an occasional eye on the actual cards being played!

Section 1 – The Basics

The fundamental formats

Five-Card Draw (a.k.a. "Real" Poker, Straight Poker)

Playing: Ante. Deal each player five cards. Bet.* In turn, each player "draws" (exchanges) between zero and three cards from their hand—up to four, with an Ace—for fresh cards from the deck. Another bet. Everyone shows what they have.

> *The player to the dealer's left starts the action each time.*

Forming the Hand: The hands rank from low to high:

Your Cards	What You've Got	How You'd Call It
A♠ 2♥ 3♣ 4♣ 6♦	High Card/Schmaltz	"Ace-high."
8♣ 8♦ K♦ 9♥ 3♠	A Pair	"Pair o' Snowmen."
A♦ A♥ 6♠ 6♥ 2♣	Two Pair	"Aces Up."
10♠ 10♣ 10♥ 3♦ 5♦	Three of a Kind	"Trip 10s."
7♥ 8♦ 9♣ 10♠ J♦	A Straight	"Jack-high Straight."
4♦ 10♦ 8♦ Q♦ 7♦	A Flush	"Queen-high Flush."
5♠ 5♥ 5♣ K♥ K♦	A Full House	"Boat, 5s full of Kings."
9♣ 9♠ 9♦ 9♥ 3♣	Four of a Kind	"Two Pair, 9s...and 9s." **
10♣ J♣ Q♣ K♣ A♣	A Straight-Flush	"I've got a Royal!"

Tip: In Poker, all suits are equal. Thus in the rare case of two players having identically ranked but differently suited five-card winning hands, they'd split the pot.

**Part of the fun of a great hand is revealing it in a coy, cocky way like this. But try to restrain yourself, even around friends. No one likes a sore winner!

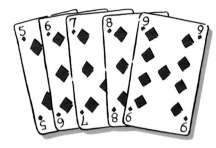

The Reasoning Behind the Game: Drawing cards can improve one's hand. Generally, discarding three means a player has a Pair; two signifies Trips or a Pair and a "kicker" (high card); and one is usually a Straight or Flush attempt.

Winning: Two Pair will likely win.

Example: You're dealt 7♣ J♦ 7♠ 7♥ 3♠. Three 7s is a good start, but vulnerable since it's not likely to improve. When the action gets to you, check if possible; otherwise, simply call the bet. You don't want to scare away any weaker hands and a big bet or raise won't scare away any stronger hands. Rather than two cards, just discard the 3♠. You can ignore the remote possibility of picking up the "case" (fourth) 7; and it won't affect your chances of landing a Full House. Regardless of what card you draw, just check and/or call the second bet. If you win, you'll get more money in the pot that way. And if you lose, you won't have put as much in!

"The Call of the Wild"

Calling wild cards is popular not only because they can represent any cards that will help a player's hand, but also because of all their fun nicknames. For example, "Suicide Kings and Snowmen" refers to the King of Hearts, King of Diamonds, and all four 8s. (See the glossary for other colorful card terms.) Wild cards can also be built in to the rules of a game (see "Baseball" in Section 6). Additionally, they can be determined in Stud games when matching cards, sequential cards, or cards that add up to a certain number appear. The problem with multiple wilds in any game is that it's too easy to get good hands. And that sends the natural balance of hand rankings right into the trash, probably why calling mostly games with wilds is known as "Trash Poker."

Strategy: After seeing every other player bet and exchange cards, the dealer has the advantage here. So bet based on your position. If you're early to act, play strong or fold. If you're late, it's okay to limp in with less. As in all poker, if you don't have it and can't fake it, you should get out!

Options & Variations:

- Use a "qualifier," as in "Jacks or Better, Trips to Win" (Section 11) or add "wild" cards (as featured in the sidebar to the left).
- Section 3 is dedicated to other types of Draw alternatives.

Five-Card Stud

Do they have it or don't they?

Playing: Ante. Deal each player a "hole" card (face-down*) and "up" card (face-up). Bet.** Each of the last three rounds, deal each player an additional up card and bet. After the fourth bet, flip the hole cards and determine a winner.

The Reasoning Behind the Game: More visible hands and more betting.

Winning: Two Pair—or even a high Pair—could win the game.

Example: You have a hand containing [6♦] 6♠ J♣ (the bracketed one is your hole card). Unfortunately, another player has two 10s showing. Don't give up, it's the perfect time for a bluff! Bet strong into the 10s. The other player will either guess you have a Jack in the hole or figure out that you are bluffing. Either way it is okay as you still have two chances to pair the Jack or to get another 6. And even if you get caught failing, that player will be more likely to call you later, when you might actually have the better hand!

Strategy: With up to 80 percent of players' hands showing, the dealer's advantage dwindles. Thus, whoever is the most skilled, both at implying what they have and inferring what others have will do well. Pay attention to how players react to their cards and how they bet. It's a great chance to read their play.

Options & Variations:
• "Seven-Card Stud" is the most famous variation, but a plethora of other popular adaptations appear throughout the book.

*The hole card can be peeked at, but must remain face-down on the table throughout the hand.

**In each round of Stud games, the player with the best hand showing leads the bet. If two players have identical high cards/hands showing, whoever received theirs first bets first.

"Wishful Thinking"

Home poker players tend to be overly optimistic. For instance, consider if you had [6♦] 7♥ 8♠ 10♠ against an opponent showing Trip 8s. Are you even thinking of staying in? Your last card could be a 9, filling your inside Straight. But there are no other cards that could possibly make your hand better than Three of a Kind! The smart, realistic play would be to fold.

Seven-Card Stud

More betting and possibilities.

Playing: Ante. Deal each player two down, one up. Bet. Each of the next three rounds, deal each player an additional up card and bet. Deal the final card down, bet, and reveal the hands (to see who wins).

Forming the Hand: Still just your best five.

The Reasoning Behind the Game: Receiving two extra cards creates twenty additional hand combinations, which, along with the typically bigger pots, provides a compelling reason for players to stay in.

Winning: High Trips are usually sufficient (in the absence of the occasional Straight, Flush, or Full House).

Example: On Fifth Street* you have [4♣ 8♣] 7♣ 3♦ J♣. Your Flush draw** is a little vulnerable, but don't bet the minimum. And don't default to the maximum. Bet 75 cents. It's a confusing, middle-of-the-road bet that should get anyone with Two Pair up through a Straight draw thinking twice. By varying your bets in each context, you'll be a more mysterious, less readable player—a solid strategic benefit!

Strategy: It's obvious that more cards equals more chances for better hands. But many beginners focus solely on the possibilities within their own hands, without considering those of their

"Getting the Most from Your Monster"

In a game where Two Pair normally wins, a Full House or Four of a Kind is a "monster." The best way to take advantage of this virtually assured win is to "slowplay" the hand. In other words, don't raise. Bet humbly so as not to scare anyone away. At least until the end, when you unleash your Frankenstein and collect the handsome pot from the innocent villagers.

Best Five out of Seven

Since many of the games throughout the book are played with seven cards, here are some examples of how to figure your strongest quintet subset:

Your Cards	Your Best Five	What You've Got
8♠ Q♠ 8♥ Q♣ 6♦ 8♣ Q♦	Q♠ Q♣ Q♦ 8♠ 8♥	A Full House
5♥ K♠ J♦ 10♣ J♥ K♦ 5♣	K♠ K♦ J♦ J♥ 10♣	Two Pair
A♠ 2♠ 10♠ 3♠ 9♠ 4♣ 7♠	A♠ 10♠ 9♠ 7♠ 3♠	A Flush
4♦ 7♠ J♣ 6♥ 2♣ 8♥ 5♦	4♦ 5♦ 6♥ 7♠ 8♥	A Straight
8♣ 9♣ 10♥ J♥ A♥ 3♥ 4♠	A♥ J♥ 10♥ 9♣ 8♣	Nothing
3♦ J♦ 2♦ 6♦ 8♦ 5♦ 4♦	2♦ 3♦ 4♦ 5♦ 6♦	A Straight-Flush
7♥ 7♠ 7♣ A♥ A♦ 4♠ 7♦	7♥ 7♠ 7♣ 7♦ A♥	Four of a Kind
6♣ 8♣ 9♣ 10♣ A♦ 8♦ 5♥	8♣ 8♦ A♦ 10♣ 9♣	A Pair
Q♦ A♥ K♠ Q♣ J♣ 9♦ Q♥	Q♦ Q♣ Q♥ A♥ K♠	Three of a Kind

opponents. Think about how likely it is that even if you improve, another player could still beat you. A big part of playing "tight" (disciplined) is knowing when to gracefully bow out of battles you can't win.

Options & Variations:
- "Follow the Queen" (Section 10), "Baseball" (Section 6), "High-Low," and "Chicago" (both Section 2) are the best-known offshoots.

*The "street" refers to the card/betting round, in this case after the third up card's dealt.

**When used as a noun, "draw" refers to a hand that needs more cards to be complete, in this case, another Club to make a Flush.

Criss-Cross*

Common cards going this way and that.

Not to be confused with "Stonehenge" (a.k.a. "Iron Cross") in Section 6.

Playing: Ante. Deal each player four cards. Deal five additional cards face-down in the shape of a cross. Bet. Each of the next four rounds, flip one of the cross's outside cards and rotate the starting bettor. Reveal the middle card last, bet, and "showdown" (compare hands).

Forming the Hand: The best five from the four in your hand plus the three in either the row or the column. Consecutive outside cards of the cross cannot be used.

The Reasoning Behind the Game: Since players will use between one and three cards from one of the lines, the revelation of the cross is designed to keep faithful players in for a majority of the six betting rounds.

Winning: As with all community card games, what wins depends on what turns up. If cards to a Straight or Flush don't show, Two Pair is probably good enough. A Pair in the row or column means a Full House is that much likelier.

5♠

10♣ 4♦ 10♦

A♥

Example: You've got 10♣ 2♥ 3♦ A♦ in your hand and the cross on the left. You almost have a Full House, but the Ace is out of place in the column. You also almost have a Diamond Flush. But hey, using the column you do have a 5-high Straight. Definitely your best hand—and a possible winner.

Strategy: First, be careful in forming and calling your hand! And second, don't place too much value on the middle card. Newbies sometimes wait through five rounds of betting even if the mystery card couldn't help their hand to be a contender! Practiced players avoid that misdirection and look more to the outside cards to make their hands. They also pay close attention to players' reactions and how they bet after each card is revealed.

Options & Variations:
- Super-Cross, Criss-Cross's big brother, deals two cards to each player, but offers a row and column both five cards long (again, revealed from the outside spiraling in).
- Section 4 is teeming with other community card games.

Two-Card Guts (a.k.a. Drops, Balls)

Pair of cajones required. (Figuratively, anyway.)

Playing: Ante $1. Every player is dealt two cards, evaluates them, and holds them face-down a few inches above the table. The dealer orders, "1...2...3...Drop!" All players hold their cards (to stay in) or drop them (to bypass the round).

Forming the Hand: No Straights or Flushes. Just a Pair...or not.

The Reasoning Behind the Game: With no conventional betting, it's less about skill and more about nerves.

Winning: If only one person holds, they win the pot and the game is over. Otherwise, whoever held with the highest hand takes the pot; everyone else who held pays the pot $2; and anyone who dropped either re-antes $1 or is out for the rest of the game. The winner each round is likely to have a Pair, an Ace, and/or both cards of 10 or higher.

Example: Four rounds in, you're dealt Q♦ J♠. Not bad, but not worth holding. Having been penalized (possibly a few times), players are likely to be more selective with what they hold. Although your Queen-Jack might've had an outside chance early on, you should drop it now like a hot potato. Those $2 fines add up!

Strategy: If it's your deal, rather than a drop, call a "sequential declare." One by one, players verbally indicate whether they're in or out. The dealer, who declares last, has a distinct advantage. To be fair, if the game goes more than one round, rotate either the dealer or first declarer counterclockwise.

Options & Variations:
- Don't drop late. It's poor form—and punishable up to $5.
- Allow players to drop only three times before they're out for good.
- Limit the number of rounds. Once it's gone around the table, any money stays in for the next game.
- Keep things moving by only reshuffling when there aren't enough cards to go around.
- Extend the excitement by making it a three-win "legs" game. (See the "Nothing Beats a Great Set of Legs" sidebar in Section 10.)
- Make the losing punishment matching the pot. (This can quickly get expensive and change the mood and strategy of the game!)
- See "Additional Guts Games & Rules" in Section 12 for many other ways to play.

Three-Card Poker (a.k.a. Monte Carlo*)

And now for something completely different...

*Not to be confused with the street hustler game
"Three-Card Monte."*

Playing: It works in multiple formats: Draw
(exchanging a max of two), Stud (one down,
one up; with another up round), or Guts
(with the telltale drop).

Forming the Hand: All 22,100 possible
three-card hands rank from worst to best:

Hand	Ways to Make the Hand	Approx. Chances of Getting It with Three Cards
No Pair	16,440	74.39% (1 to 3)**
Pair	3744	16.94% (5 to 1)
Flush	1096	4.96% (19 to 1)
Straight	720	3.26% (30 to 1)
Three of a Kind	52	0.24% (424 to 1)
Straight Flush	48	0.22% (459 to 1)

**This format expresses how many times the hand won't happen as compared to how many times it will. As
opposed to the others, the number on the right is bigger for this one, since No Pair happens a majority of
the time.*

The Reasoning Behind the Game: As you can see, a hand's strength is based on how rare it is. But many players aren't familiar with the proper pecking order. So discuss it before playing.

Winning: Since two-thirds of the possible hands don't contain a Pair, any Pair has a fighting chance.

Example: You're dealt A♥ Q♣ 9♦. If playing Draw, "stand pat" (don't take any cards). Statistically you'll beat a majority of hands—and your boldness will probably scare away some players. In Stud, bet strong. Depending on your hole card, you'll read as having either a Straight or a high Pair. In Guts, it wouldn't be the worst hand, but then again it wouldn't be the best...

Strategy: Calling the game itself as a five-card alternative is a good strategy, since the shift in game strategy can catch other players off-guard. Just be sure to distinguish it from Straight Three-Card, which ironically doesn't recognize Straights—or Flushes. It's based simply on rank. Thus 2♦ 2♣ 2♠ would beat 6♥ 6♠ 4♦, which would in turn beat K♣ Q♣ J♣. All sorts of shifts in thinking!

Options & Variations:
- Up the ante and/or minimum bets to compensate for the fewer betting rounds.
- Monte Carlo is incorporated in such other games as "3-5-7" (Section 10), "Two Plus One," and "Pass One, Draw One" (both Section 2).

Section 2 – Elementary Evolutions

Standard deviations

Two Plus One (a.k.a. Two and One)

Guts tension, Monte Carlo fun.

Playing: Ante $1 and deal each player two cards. After a Guts-styled drop, those still in flip up their cards. Each of the losers pays the player with the best hand $1. Deal each competitor a third card down. Bet. Reveal the winner.

Forming the Hand: The first round is just High Card and Pairs. The second round can include Flushes and Straights.

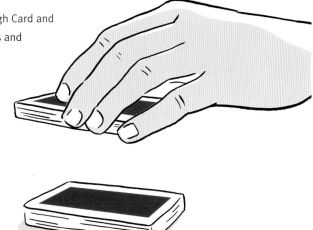

The Reasoning Behind the Game: Paying the $1 penalty punishes those players who were avoiding a first round fold as they were waiting for the big payoff. By defini-tion, the player who wins the first round will lead the second round betting.

Winning: A hand like A♣ 7♦ could proba-bly win in the first round, but not in the second (without pairing the Ace). Likewise, J♥ 6♥ 3♥ isn't shabby, but none of its possible two-card starting hands would be worth holding. (Higher) Pairs are a safer bet all around.

Example: Your 8♠ 9♠ seems somewhat promising for the second round, but you'll almost certainly owe someone money in the first round. If it were just a Straight or Flush draw, it probably wouldn't be worth it. But with both (and the Straight-Flush draw), it's probably worth investing the extra dollar.

Strategy: Chase Flushes and Straights only after considering the big picture. Look for holdings with multiple second round Pair, Flush, and Straight possibilities.

Options & Variations:
- Deal the third card up, skip the betting, and go right to showdown.
- Instead of a fixed-limit penalty, make the worst first-round hand match the pot.
- "3-5-7" (Section 10) has a similar dynamic. Also see "Additional Guts Games & Rules" (Section 12).

Lowball (a.k.a. Lowboy)

Hope for the worst!

Playing: This feature can be applied to any format (Draw, Stud, Guts, or Community). The goal in getting the worst five cards (according to the standard five-card hand rankings) is to avoid any Pairs, Straights, or Flushes and have the lowest high card. Therefore, a "Perfect Low" is A-2-3-4-6 of different suits.

Forming the Hand: Normally, the top two cards define the hand. For instance, an A♥ 2♦ 3♣ 5♥ 6♥ is a "6-5 Low" and an A♦ 2♣ 3♦ 4♠ 7♥ is a "7-4 Low." Although, technically a player with the first hand would need to say only that they had a "6 Low" to indicate they had the second player (with a "7 Low") beat.

"Uninventing the Wheel"

In casino poker, Straights (6♠ 5♥ 4♣ 3♦ 2♦) and Flushes (7♣ 4♣ 3♣ 2♣ A♣) don't count against Lows. Therefore, the casino says these first two hands are great Lows and the best one possible is a 5-4-3-2-A (a.k.a. a "bicycle" or "wheel") of any suits. True, 5 is lower than 6. But since the best Low is partly defined as the "worst High," Straights and/or Flushes cannot be ignored! It may seem weird to an avid casino player that a non-suited 6-4 reigns supreme, but that's how Lows work at the kitchen table—unless the dealer/host proclaims otherwise.

Any hand with an 8 or higher or at least a Pair would lose to either of those hands.

The Reasoning Behind the Game: It gives players something different to shoot for.

Winning: In games with only five cards, an 8-7 could win; with seven cards, it'd probably take a 7-5; with three cards, it varies.

Example: Your [5♣ Q♠] A♦ 3♥ 10♥ 6♣ is battling a [X X]* J♥ 6♠ 2♦ 5♥. Time for a probe. Bet big. If player 2 quickly calls or raises, they probably have an Ace-3 or Ace-4 in the hole. Since only a 2 on Seventh Street could help you win or tie, you should fold faster than a greased accordion. But if player 2 hesitates to call, he might have only one low card in the hole. Stay in, bet like you've already got a Perfect Low, and hope that he pairs up and you don't on the last card!

Strategy: Statistically, more than half the five-card hands dealt don't have a Pair. Thus, if you have a Pair, the only reasons not to fold would be if it's hidden (either both in the hole or one down and one up) or if it's a game with more than five cards.

Options & Variations:
• If Aces are established as high-only, 7-5-4-3-2 is the best possible (Kansas City Lowball) hand.

An "X" denotes an unknown card.

"Here, Piggy, Piggy"

Going "pig" means a player in a "split" game is greedily attempting to win both halves of the pot. In a five-card game, a player can't do this unless "wheels" are allowed or everyone else folds. In games with more cards, players may use different sets of five to go each way. For instance, a player might go pig in Seven-Card Stud with [5♦ 10♣] A♦ 3♥ 4♣ 6♥ [7♥]—a 7-high Straight, and 6-5 Low. A player must win both ways in order to be successful. Obviously, if the pig loses both directions, the two best hands split the pot. But if the pig loses in one direction, the player with the best hand in the other direction automatically wins the whole pot—unless "doorknobs" are allowed. An example of this would be if players with a Flush and an 8 Low stayed in against the above hand. The player with the Flush would kill the pig and win half the pot; and the player with the 8 Low—for staying in, despite being second best—would back into the other half of the pot. Finally, despite the fact that a tie isn't a win, some people give a pig winning one way and tying the other three-fourths of the pot as a compromise.

High-Low

Enter "Plan B" into your Poker vocabulary...

Playing: As with "Lowball" (just above), this feature can be applied to any format (Draw, Stud, Guts, Community) with any number of cards.

The Reasoning Behind the Game: It offers players a second way to win if the first doesn't work out.

Winning: The highest and lowest hands divide the pot evenly. If the pot doesn't split evenly, the High hand gets the extra chip.

"Well, I Do Declare"

High-Low (and other split games) can end several ways. First is no declare or "the cards speak" (for themselves). After the final bet, all the cards are revealed and the best hands in either direction win. Second is a sequential declare in which, starting to the dealer's left, each player verbally indicates they're going High, Low, or Both. This gives a large advantage to those in late position. Third and most popular is a chip declare.

At the same time, all players take chips in their hands and bring them under the table. The mantra is chanted: "One for Low, Two for High, Three for Both"—we add "Four for Phil," playing off a math error a cohort once made. In any case, every player brings one closed fist above the table and on the dealer's signal reveals his chip(s) at the same time. This is a clear, fair way of determining who's in direct competition with whom.

If all players declare the same way, there's just a bet and reveal as usual. If a sole player declares in one direction, it's known as a lock. In other words, that player doesn't have any competition and is guaranteed half the pot. If there's a lock in both directions, the two players simply split the pot. But if there's a lock in one direction and not the other, a problem arises: Any betting done by the lock might be seen as selfish and greedy. Several possible solutions are:

1 Bet as usual. Implying there isn't a problem.
2 The lock starts the bet. It will most likely be the maximum. If anyone raises, the lock can raise back. Otherwise, it just goes around once, the lock having happily built up the pot.
3 The lock can't raise. As usual, the player with the best hand showing starts the bet. The lock can only call, but the pot still gets padded a little.
4 Bet only if there's no lock. Seemingly fair—unless you're the lock!
5 Never bet after the declare, avoiding the problem altogether.

Because of the very different ways to handle the situation, before it becomes an issue, always ask if there's a bet after the declare!

Example: You end up with [A♠ 10♠] 2♦ 3♠ 4♠ 6♥ [8♠]. You read Low (and have an unbeatable one). But that Spade Flush is a nice, well-hidden High! Go pig unless another player shows Trips or a Pair and is betting heavily (either indicating a possible Full House). Better to go just Low and win half, than be a hog and risk getting nothing!

Strategy: As a rule, declare in the direction you most likely read. Obviously, with [10♦] 7♠ K♣ K♠ 7♥ you'd read/declare High. But what about with [X] 3♥ 4♠ 5♣ 7♦? It could be either a Straight or a decent Low. In that case, you'd read as going in whichever direction has the least/weakest competition. If no one showed a high Pair or possible Straight, you'd go High; if no one showed better than a 7-5 Low, you'd go that way—regardless of your hole card!

Options & Variations:

- Sometimes a "qualifier" is used to determine if the game will be High-Low or one or the other, such as in "Sixty-Four" (mentioned in "The Over/Under" sidebar in Section 11), "Omaha" (Section 10), and "Jacks or Back" (a version of "Jacks or Better, Trips to Win" mentioned in Section 11).

Roll Your Own (a.k.a. Mexican Stud*)

Hands-on, do-it-yourself Stud.

Not to be confused with "Mexican Poker" or "Spanish Poker."

Playing: Starting with two in Five-Card Stud and three in Seven-Card Stud, deal each player all their cards face-down. Each round after the cards are dealt, every player flips a down card—except for Seven-Card Stud's last card, which stays down. Bet as usual.

The Reasoning Behind the Game: Players typically try to disguise their hands, weak for strong and/or Low for High (in High-Low). But the worst disguise of all is playing it straightforward!

Example: Some possible ways to play various Seven-Card Stud High-Low hands:

What You Have	What to Roll	Why
[3♠ K♦ 4♠]	The King	The odd card is typically shown first.
[5♠ J♦ 8♠] 10♥	The 5 or 8	If a player already shows a Jack, yours is inside information.
[J♥ 10♣ A♥] 5♥	The 10	It hides the possible Flush.
[9♣ 4♦ 2♥] 6♣ 3♣	The 9	It flexibly favors your weaker (High) option.
[4♣ 5♣ 6♦] 8♦ 7♥ 4♥	The 5	If 6s are showing in others' hands, it'll lure in players who think you're bluffing the Straight.
[7♠ Q♦ 3♣] Q♠ 7♦ 7♣	The Queen or 3	The Queen will have players second-guessing your possible Full House. The 3 will blindside them altogether!

Strategy: Be open to changing your plan midstream. Bluff. Vary your "rules" and style enough from game to game to be a difficult read. And finally, be wary of any player who stays in with what looks like garbage, when better stuff is clearly showing in others' hands!

Options & Variations:

- In Dakota, it's assumed you roll Seventh Street, unless you pay a predetermined fee to keep it down.
- In Shifting Sands, the first card the player rolls is wild throughout that player's hand. Similar to "Kankakee," in which each player's first card dealt up is wild.

- In Five-Card Stud, Monterrey makes the hole card and any matching cards in the player's hand wild. Similar to "Low Card in the Hole" (Section 10) in Seven-Card Stud.
- In Seven-Card Stud, Flip speeds up the process by dealing players four cards and having them flip two (effectively skipping a round).
- Similarly, Boston Roll 'Em deals four, but has players discard one and flip one before the first bet.
- For even more drama, see "Blind Stud" (Section 8).

Pass a Card, Buy a Card (a.k.a. Take It or Leave It)

Money might buy you happiness.

Playing: Deal the down cards as per usual Stud. Start each up round by dealing a card face-up to the player to the dealer's left. If he likes it, he keeps it. Otherwise, player one pays a 25-cent fee, passes the card to his left and gets a deck card he has to keep.* The next player can keep whatever card he's passed or dealt, or pay 'n' pass as well. The action continues clockwise to the dealer, who either accepts or "buries" (under the deck, out of play) a card. End each round with a bet.

The Reasoning Behind the Game: Each player has a chance to improve and/or redeem their hand each round. Making this a definite dealer advantage game and a natural for High-Low.

Winning: Expect to see Straights in Three-Card, Trips in Five-Card, and possibly Full Houses in Seven-Card. The Lows will be comparably good.

Nothing's worse than being dealt the same card you just paid to pass! Because of the uncanny ability of Dave Manalan (who plays in my dad's game) to torture players in this way when dealing, this phenomena is known as "getting Manalan'ed."

Example: In Five-Card High-Low with [Q♠] K♣ 10♦ J♦ 4♥, you debate whether to pass the 4 into an [X] 3♥ 6♠ 2♣. Since you're clearly not going Low, don't worry about that end. Instead, focus on answering:

- How many 9s and Aces are still in the deck (to make your Straight)?
- How many people are still in?
- How many of those players look like they're going High?
- If another card pairs you up, could 10s or better win High?
- How many 5s are out? (You could be giving player two a Straight!)

Strategy: It's tempting to get caught up in the passing and buying, but try to avoid buying your way into second place. Also, you can't force a hand to go Low if it wants to go High. Take a few freebies here and there and don't fight the cards.

Options & Variations:

- Increase the passing price each round.
- Double/triple the rate to pass into a Pair/Trips.
- Push 'n' Roll (a.k.a. Puttin' Marmalade on the Pooch) has passing and buying, but deals all the cards face-down and flips them in unison right before each round's bet.
- Pass One, Draw One (a.k.a. The Kennebunk Shuffle) deals players three. They must pass one in the next round, but may draw a card in the final round.
- See the common addendum "...With a Buy in the End" in Section 11.
- See similar "shopping" games in Section 5.

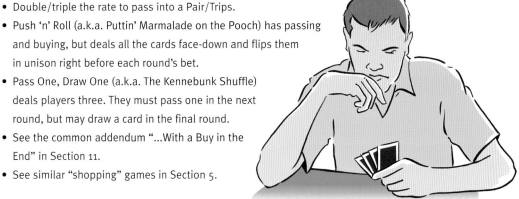

Chicago

Tottlin' town and suit-based Stud game.

Playing: The High hand splits the pot with the highest Spade in the hole.

The Reasoning Behind the Game: Players with otherwise lousy hands hope to win half the pot by catching a stray Spade.

Winning: The Highs are per regular Stud. The high Spade depends on how many players stay in, etc., but tends to be 10 or higher.

Example: You're dealt [9♦ A♠] 3♣. Since you're guaranteed half, your goal is to get as much money as possible into the pot. Don't make any big bets or raises unsubstantiated by what you have showing. You'll scare away the Spade-seekers and wind up just trading chips with the player going High.

Strategy: Keep track of every Spade you see. For instance, if you've seen the Ace, King, and 10, you know your Jack in the hole is powerful. By the way, don't "try" for high Spade. It's a real newbie move!

Options & Variations:

- In Low Chicago (a.k.a. Cleveland), the low Spade (decide whether it's the Ace or 2) in the hole grabs half the pot.
- To make it harder for players to back into the pot, use a declare ("One chip for Spade, Two for High, or Three for Both") and/or a qualifier. For example, a player going Spade must have at least a (certain) Pair.
- In Murder (1), the High splits the pot with the highest natural Spade up or down; the Queen of Spades dealt down is wild; and dealt up, she resets the hand. Immediately stop play, collect the cards, re-ante, and re-deal until her majesty doesn't show up.
- See "Illinois" (a.k.a. "Black Mariah (2)") and "Royal Chicago" in Section 12, which take "Chicago" to the next level.

SECTION 3 – The Art of the Draw

Some sketchy alternatives

No Draw

Even more straightforward than straight poker!

Playing: Ante. Deal each player five cards. Bet (without discarding). Showdown.

The Reasoning Behind the Game: Just luck and a little bluffing.

Winning: A decent Pair could win.

Example: Regardless of your cards, when it's your bet, pause momentarily and raise the maximum. Then—this is the important part—take note of each player's reaction and consequential action. Who folded? Who twitched, but stayed in? Who re-raised? And what kinds of hands did those players have? You can learn valuable information about who's bluffable and who isn't.

Strategy: In Indian Poker, you have no idea what card you have held/stuck to your forehead, but you surmise based on how folks look at you. Here you can't see others' cards, but you can see your own. In both cases, you need to disregard your cards to some degree and play the other players.

Options & Variations:
• At least double the usual ante to make up for the single round of (likely tentative) betting.

All for One or One for All (a.k.a. Five to One)

Ready, musketeers?

Playing: Ante. Deal each player five. Bet. Each player can stand pat, draw one card, or exchange all five! Bet and reveal.

The Reasoning Behind the Game: The implied game logic:

Your Starting Hand	What You Do
No Pair (or Straight or Flush draw)	Fold. Drawing five to a Pair is fairly likely to happen, but not to win.
Four to a Straight or Flush	Draw one.
Any Pair	Discard your lowest card. If the draw doesn't improve your hand, get ready to fold.
Three of a Kind	Stand pat.* It's a power move and you might win without any help.
Anything better than Three of a Kind	Stand pat, unless it's with Four of a Kind.
Four of a Kind	Draw one to bait everyone.

* This advice is purposefully different from that given back in Five-Card Draw's example because the object is to keep players guessing. It wouldn't be wrong here to draw a card—or two. This is just one alternative.

Winning: Two Pair or Three of a Kind is likely to win.

Example: You are dealt 9♠ 10♣ 10♦ J♠ Q♦. Since you have just as good a chance of picking up an 8 or King as you do of pairing up the Jack or Queen (for Two Pair), split up the 10s and then go for the open-ended Straight. It is more likely to win if it hits.

Strategy: You could win with a fresh hand, but don't fall for the gimmick of exchanging all five cards.

Options & Variations:

- With more than five players you may run out of cards. Agree ahead of time whether it's okay to shuffle and draw from the discards.

Shotgun

A more drawn-out Draw.

Playing: Ante. Deal each player three cards. Bet. Deal each player another card. Bet. Another card. Bet. A standard draw. Bet and reveal.

The Reasoning Behind the Game: More suspense, but the betting tends to be tentative or unsubstantiated.

Winning: The hands should be similar to regular Five-Card Draw.

Example: You're dealt A♠ 3♠ 4♥. Bet the longshot Straight and possible Flush modestly. Next, the Q♣ — no help. Check, if possible. Then the 8♦ — less help. Check again. Keeping the Ace-Queen, you draw 7♥ 4♦ Q♥. It may not seem like much, but a Pair of Ladies with an Ace kicker could win. Bet it like it

was Three of a Kind and the others might believe.

Strategy: Instead of guessing what might win, focus on folding what might lose: Lower, more spread-out, and/or non-suited cards without pairs, such as 10♣ 7♦ 2♥. Shoot it early and put it out of its misery.

Options & Variations:

- Pig Stud deals the fourth and fifth cards face-up—which is how they remain until it's time for the draw, when it becomes an all-closed game again (with the players holding all their cards).
- In Double-Barreled Shotgun, after the draw, players expose four cards (one at a time) and bet as in Stud. This makes for eight rounds of betting.

"The Dealer's Dilemma"

Calling an entertaining game is nice, but ultimately you want to give yourself an advantage. The best games for that are ones where players make visible decisions. For instance, in "Italian Poker" (just below), "Do Ya?," and "Nickel, Dime, Quarter" (both Section 5), players see two or three up cards. As the dealer, you get to see what choices everyone makes, plus more overall cards in the process, making your eventual decision a more educated one. The only catch is that those games typically have rotating betting and other offbeat options that'll keep you busy as a dealer. And therefore, a little distracted as a player.

Italian Poker

You'll get an offer you can't necessarily use.

Playing: Ante. Deal each player five cards (down). Bet. Deal two cards face-up—sliding the second partially under the first. Offer the two to the player to the dealer's immediate left, who has only three options:

1 Take none
2 Take just the top card
3 Take both cards

If the player wants the top or both cards, he discards one or two face-down and takes it/them. With cards from the deck, either replace both offer cards or slide a new one under the old bottom card. Proceed clockwise until each player has had a two-card offer. Final bet. The best hand wins.

The Reasoning Behind the Game: As in "Pass a Card, Buy a Card" (Section 2) or "Bunkbeds" (Section 4), players are plagued by the fact that their choice is limited. In this case, they can't just take the bottom card. It's a mental distraction that becomes an advantage for anyone who's played the game and understands the dynamic.

Winning: Two Pair may win, but beware of Straights, Flushes, and Full Houses—oh my!

Example: Consider how a 4♣ [top] 7♣ [bottom] offer might affect a starting hand of Two Pair, such as 7♦ 7♠ 10♦ 10♥ 2♥. Unfortunately, you couldn't swap that bottom 7 for the 2 to make a Full House. But by taking both and breaking up the 10s, you would improve to Three of a Kind (4♣ 7♣ 7♦ 7♠ 10♦).

Strategy: When you first play, focus on whether what could help you is offered. When you're comfortable with that, note anyone who takes both cards. If they can't fill a Straight or Flush, assume they're for Two Pair or a Full House, which should become apparent when the player bets. Finally, when it all makes sense, you'll be able to process the implications of every card each player does/doesn't take.

Options & Variations:
- Play it High-Low.
- Roll the cards at the end a la "Anaconda" (Section 6), to add more betting.
- Implement a pricing structure, such as: The Top for 75 cents or Both for $1. Or add a cost to the cards to allow just the bottom to be taken: The Top for 25 cents, the Bottom for 75 cents, or Both for $1.
- See Section 5 for other multiple-option games.

Psycho

Five-Card Draw shockingly transforms into Seven-Card Stud.

Playing: Ante. Deal each player five cards. Bet. Draw. Bet. All at once, players turn up three cards from their hands. Bet. Deal each player an up card. Bet. Deal each player a final down card. Bet and reveal.

The Reasoning Behind the Game: This allows players to make their hands from as many as ten cards—implying a max of only five players.

Winning: Two Pair may win, but the occasional Straight, Flush, or Full House hits.

Example: You're dealt 8♦ J♠ 9♠ 10♥ 2♣. Instead of instinctually tossing the 2, hold onto it. When you flip the 9-10-Jack and bet like you have a Straight, players may think you were dealt a pat hand. In the meantime, you still have a pretty good chance to pick up a 7 or Queen in the last two cards. Just don't look too anxious!

Strategy: Pay close attention to how many cards players draw. Three still indicates a Pair. But drawing two may be an attempt at a Straight or Flush. It can be tough to tell, so also factor in what three cards they flip up and assume they're the player's strongest.

Options & Variations:
- Play it High-Low.
- Limit the maximum number of cards drawn to allow for more players.
- Instead of flipping all three at once, do it one at a time, to increase the number of bets.

English Stud

Six-Card Stud with three optional draws.

Playing: Ante. Deal each player one down, one up. Bet. Deal Third Street up. Bet. Deal Fourth Street up. Bet. Give each player the option to exchange any one of their cards. Bet. Deal Fifth Street up. Bet. Similar optional exchanges. Bet. Deal Sixth Street down. Bet. Optional exchanges. Bet and reveal.

The Reasoning Behind the Game: Replace up cards (costing 50 cents) up and down cards (costing 75 cents) down. As compared to Five-Card Stud, there are four additional cards and twice as many bets.

Winning: With players potentially seeing nine cards, expect Straights and Flushes High and at least a 7 Low.

Example: Before the final trade in High-Low, you've got [A♠] 6♦ A♥ 6♣ 3♣ [2♥]. Against only one or two other Highs, you might trade the 2 to fill the House. Otherwise, trading the pocket Ace and hoping for a 4 or 5 sets you up for a nice Low—and leaves people guessing which way you're going in the process.

Strategy: Don't automatically purchase three additional cards. Hands that need that much help aren't worth chasing and will have you second guessing yourself the whole way—especially in High-Low. Use the extra cards wisely to up your chances of attaining something specific. Recognize and fold "nothing" (e.g., two high and two low cards in the first four). And always be mindful of what others are drawing to.

Options & Variations:
- Deal it two down, three up, one down to greatly change the dynamic of the game.
- Each round, rotate the first right to exchange.
- Adjust the number of cards and exchanges based on the number of players.

Spit (in the Ocean)

Four-Card Draw with a community card.

Playing: Ante. Deal each player four cards. Deal a community card face-down. Bet. Each player can exchange up to two cards. Bet. The community card is revealed. Bet and showdown.

Forming the Hand: Use the four in your hand plus the one on the table to make your best five.

The Reasoning Behind the Game: The draw gives everyone hope. The community card gives everyone information—and a little tension. It's a card everyone must use, yet no one knows until the end.

Winning: Two Pair is often all it takes.

Example: You're dealt 6♥ 7♠ 8♣ 9♣. Play this tight. With little betting, wait to see if the community card is a 5 or 10. If anyone bets the max and/or raises, fold. Your only backup is a Pair that won't likely win.

Strategy: With a Pair and two low cards (6 or less), draw two. Never draw more than one to a Straight or Flush. And if you're dealt Trips, stand pat.

Options & Variations:

• If the community card and other three like it are made wild, a Full House may win, if just the three like it (but not the community card itself) are wild, Trips could win.

• In Phlegm (in the Ocean), after revealing the community card, each of the last three rounds, players turn up one card from their hands and bet.

• Stormy Weather uses three community cards. After the draw, reveal the community cards one at a time and bet. Players may incorporate only one of the community cards into their hands. As opposed to Cincinnati, which deals four community cards and allows players to use any five of the eight.

SECTION 4 – Pillars of the Community

Common games based on common cards.

Tip: The cards on the table are interchangeably referred to as "common," "shared," or "community" cards. And collectively as "the widow," "the field," or "the board."

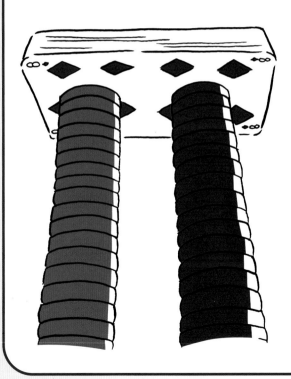

Playing: Ante. Deal cards to the players and widow. Bet. Flip a (set of) community card(s). Bet. Continue flipping cards and betting until the entire board is revealed. Bet and showdown. (Keep this template in mind when viewing all the games in the tables on pages 48 and 49.)

The Reasoning Behind the Game: In addition to providing an interesting format, community games conserve cards. For example, only seven players can play Seven-Card Stud with a regulation deck. But theoretically, three times as many could play a hand of "Texas Hold 'Em."

Winning: Many of these games are ideal for High-Low, which allows players going both ways to use different combinations of hand/board cards. The winning Highs and Lows will get increasingly better as the number of possible hand combos goes

"Fall Into Formation"

What do these common common-card games have in common?

1. A certain number of cards is dealt to each player's hand and onto the table. As long as players receive their cards face-down, one at a time in proper order, the common cards can be dealt before, during, or after.
2. The game's name normally defines the widow's shape.
3. The cards are often turned up in a prescribed order. Key cards in the middle or at intersections are saved for last, in order to preserve the mystery and keep players in.
4. The starting bettor typically rotates each round, as with other closed games, to keep things fair.
5. Rules based on the widow's geometry dictate how players form their hands. Many of the games are based on a total of seven cards. The method and number of possible configurations between the hand and board can create confusion.
6. Players more familiar with all these factors have a distinct advantage.

up. For games with five or more combos, if the board shows a possible Straight, Flush, or Full House with six or seven players, someone probably has it.

Example: In a game of High-Low Z, you're dealt Q♦ 2♠ A♦ 10♥ 3♣ and the board shows the cards in the figure on the right. The other players have been trying to somehow forge a Flush from the 9-4 row or spot a Straight in the 4-8 diagonal or 8-Jack row. But you've managed to catch the "nut" (best possible) Low, using that 4-8 diagonal. Maybe an 8-4 Low isn't the best elsewhere, but it can't be beat here. As soon as both the 8 and 4 were revealed, you should've check-raised—if allowed in your game. And on the last bet (after the declare), you should've bet the maximum allowed.

9♣ 4♠
8♣ J♦

Strategy: Immediately figure out what community cards could help your hand enough to stay in. For instance, if a fourth Spade to your Flush doesn't appear in the first two cards revealed, you'll fold, sit back, and perceptively people watch!

Options & Variations:

• Games that deal players four cards and use three from the board:

Game/Formation	Board Cards	Players Can Use...	Intersects	Combos
(Death) Wheel (a.k.a. Wheel of Fortune, Merry Go Round)	6-8	Any three consecutive cards in the circle	N/A	6-8
Pyramid (1) (a.k.a. Triangle)	6	Any side of the Pyramid	3	3
Y	7	Any of the Y's spokes	1	3
H (a.k.a. The H-Bomb)	7	The middle row, either column or either diagonal	3	5
Elevator (in the "H" formation)	7	Same as H, plus either the top or bottom row*	7	7
Bingo** (a three by three grid)	9	Any of the possible rows, columns, or diagonals	9	8

*Using the middle card with either the top or bottom two cards.

**The Tic-Tac-Toe version uses the same board formation, but deals only two cards to each hand. Both games reveal a row of three, a second row of three, then the last row one by one.

Games that deal players five cards and can use two from the board:

Game	Board Formation	Rules for Adding from the Board
Z	Two slightly skewed rows of two	Can use either row or the diagonal
Bunkbeds* (a.k.a. Bedsprings, Rockleigh)	Four columns of two	Can use any column
Nick*	Four columns of two	If using a column, must use both cards plus three from the hand
Bundles*	Six or seven columns of two	If using a column, must use both cards plus three from the hand

*Reveal the cards in these games two at a time, either column by column or any two. See "Twin Beds" and its variations in Section 10.

Texas Hold 'Em

The most popular poker game on the planet.

Intro: Half the top ten best-selling gambling books*, several trendy television programs, and thousands of websites espouse the philosophy and strategy of Hold 'Em. You may want to buy, watch, and visit them after digesting this condensed home game version. Without the casino's "blinds" (forced bets right after the antes) and more cutthroat atmosphere, kitchen table Hold 'Em is noticeably more tame.

*See the "Post-Play" section for specific suggestions on helpful poker titles.

Tip: Hold 'Em's five-card widow is exposed in three rounds: "The Flop" (three cards), "The Turn" (one card), and "The River" (one card). Greenhorns deal all five face-down before the first bet and flip the cards as they go. But real cowboys leave the field barren, "burn" the top deck card (slide it face-down into the pot) after each betting round, and shoot the Flop, Turn, or River face-up straight from the deck.

Playing: Ante.* Deal each player two. Bet. Flip the Flop. Bet. Display the Turn. Bet. Expose the River. Bet. Settle.

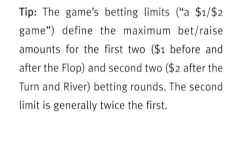

Tip: The game's betting limits ("a $1/$2 game") define the maximum bet/raise amounts for the first two ($1 before and after the Flop) and second two ($2 after the Turn and River) betting rounds. The second limit is generally twice the first.

To do blinds, the player to the dealer's left bets the "small blind" (50 cents) and the player to his left bets the "big blind" ($1). The pre-Flop bet continues to the left of the big blind. That player may call the $1, raise or fold. When the action gets around to the small blind, that player can either call the bet (for at least 50 cents more), raise, or fold. If there were no raises, the big blind doesn't need to do anything to call, but is allowed to raise himself. After the Flop, the betting returns to normal.

Forming the Hand: The best five using any from the two in your hand and the five in the field.

The Reasoning Behind the Game: These hands differ only by what two cards each player holds. Thus, it's a "pure" form of poker in the sense that it combines the quintessential skills of figuring odds, reading other players, and knowing when/how to bluff.

Winning: Statistically, the widow is almost certain to contain a Pair or three to a Straight or Flush. While Straights and Flushes do happen, Trips, Two Pair, and high Pairs win more often. It's normally played High-only.

Example: You start with 2♦ 3♦. It'd take a miracle to justify staying in. And it comes, in the form of A♣ 4♥ 5♠. You flopped a Straight! You should bet and/or raise the maximum—but not just because it's a good hand. First, players are actually likely to call your bet because they won't believe you stayed in with a lousy 2-3. Second, there's about an even chance that a 6, 7, or 8 could come on the Turn or the River, "counterfeiting" your hand (making a higher Straight possible). Still, if someone raises you, re-raise the max right back. And just pray the last two cards are both 9 or higher!

Strategy: To even begin to master "Texas Hold 'Em" requires time, skill, and dedication. Begin by learning well the eight basic concepts that follow.

1 Know what starting hands are worth keeping:
   - Any Pair (the higher the better)
   - An Ace with any other card (hoping to pair the Ace)
   - Any two cards 9 or higher (for Pairs and Straights)
   - Suited connectors (same suit, consecutive rank—at least a 6♣ 7♣, for instance—for multiple Straight and Flush opportunities)

2 Know what starting hands are worth raising. If the hand satisfies two or more of the above, raise—make it expensive for players to stay in to see a Flop!

3 Play your position. The sooner you act, the stronger your hand needs to be. If you're in an early position and your inclination is to check, you should probably fold if a bet comes to you. Conversely, if you're in a late position and you'd normally fold your cards, you may have the luxury of betting or even raising against little competition. Any holdings with both cards Jacks or higher warrant raising from any position.

4 Reevaluate your hand after the Flop. As a rule of thumb, if the Flop doesn't help you, get out—even with good cards! For example, 10♠ 10♦ is a fine start; but a Flop of 5♣ 6♣ K♣ points to a Flush draw, possibly Straight draw and at the very least a higher Pair draw.

5 Continually consider how many cards can help and hurt you. You're dealt 7♥ 8♥ and the board shows 5♥ 6♠ K♥ 2♠. Any 4, 9, or Heart on the River helps you. But if the board had shown Q♠ 6♠ K♥ 2♠ instead, any Queen, King, Jack, Ace, or Spade on the River would've hurt you. Just changing that one card made a great holding worth folding!

6 Know when you're vulnerable. If either the Turn or River will make or break your hand, you're vulnerable. (If you need both then, unfortunately, you're pathetic!) If you already have a good

hand, but someone else's hand could improve enough to beat you, you're vulnerable. In the end, if you don't have or can't make the best possible hand, you're vulnerable. Which doesn't necessarily mean you should fold (see point 8), just that you shouldn't overvalue your hand.

7   Be disciplined. Bad decisions add up over time. Even the worst hand (7♦ 2♣) has its widow (7♠ 7♥ 2♦ K♣ Q♠). But it won't win as often as A♥ K♥. You need to have a realistic feel for how likely your hand is to win decisively—and how much it'll cost you to find out.

8   Be aggressive or step aside. It's all about taking chances, but it takes a strong player to know when to fold—and be able to do it when the pressure's on. It takes a stronger player to realize the goal is to stay in with purpose and to be the one forcing others to make the tough decisions, not just letting the hand happen to them. Take control whenever possible—or, get out of the way.

Options & Variations:

- If everyone seems to stay in for the Flop, just double (or triple) the ante, skip the first bet, and go right to it.
- The "Progressive" version uses fixed betting. Players place stacks of 50 cents, $1, $1.50, and $2 in front of them. When a bet is called for, the player either folds or pushes his shortest stack into the pot.
- Instead of two, Super Eight deals three to each hand.
- Pineapple also deals three, but players discard one right before the Flop.
- Crazy Pineapple is similar, but players discard one right after the Flop.
- The Spoiler deals five, reveals the field one at a time, and discards three right before (what would've been) the Turn, making it a sort of "Cincinnati Hold 'Em."
- See "Omaha" in Section 10 for other "Hold 'Em" variations.

"The Right Bluff"

Like a strong serve in tennis, the ability to effectively bluff in poker sets the mood and pacing of the whole game. However, whereas serving is built into the routine of every tennis point, bluffing is something to try on occasion, based on considering these eight factors:

1 Your opponents' skill level. Beginners tend to blindly call bets when they shouldn't. Thus, bluffs—primarily intended to get players to fold—don't tend to work as well against them.

2 The stakes. It's tough to bluff in fixed-limit games, partially because the minimum and maximum bets can be too close together (like 25 and 50 cents). For a bluff to work, the limits need to be clearly distinguishable (like 25 cents and $2).

3 The number of bettors. Don't expect to bluff out more than two players.

4 Your position. An early position bluff could be called—or worse yet, raised—by any player(s) down the line! A large raise or re-raise from late position is more noticeable and usually better received.

5 If sandbagging is allowed, the ability to check and then raise (or re-raise) the max makes the bluff appear all the more powerful.

6 The cards showing. If you're trying to scare someone showing Straight, it helps if you're showing Flush! Otherwise, it just looks like you have a vulnerable hand and are trying to buy your way out of a bad call.

7 Your former play. If you've bluffed before and been caught, it might actually be good, unless you bluff too much or always in certain situations. The goal is for players not to be able to tell when you're bluffing!

8 Their former reactions. If it didn't work before, it most likely means that the other players either didn't pick up on it or picked up on it too well! In either case, be aware of which players and crowds your bluffs work better/worse against.

Section 5 – What's the Deal?

Buying, choosing, and using cards in irregular ways.

This or That (a.k.a. Screwin' Herman)

Decisions, decisions...

Playing: Ante. Each player is dealt two cards and discards one. Bet. Each player is dealt two more and discards one. Bet. Two more and discard. Bet. Two more and keep both. Bet and reveal. (Deal all the cards face-down.)

Forming the Hand: 5s are wild.

The Reasoning Behind the Game: The card distribution (one, one, one, two) is the reverse of regular Stud (two, one, one, one). The extra cards players see are more spread out than Draw (but still limit the number of players). The net effect is Stud-like suspense, Draw-like decisions, and a payoff filled with stress and second guessing.

Winning: Three of a Kind often wins High. Playing High-Low, use an 8 or 9 qualifier for the Low so no one goes "Low" with a Pair of 10s. Any Low that qualifies could win.

Example: In High-Low, you're dealt a 4♣ and 9♦. Keep the 4 and look to go Low. Next, a 5♣ and—it doesn't matter—keep the (wild) 5. Then a J♦ and J♠—pairs are frustrating, especially when neither card helps! So much for the Low. In round four, you're dealt 7♦ 4 ♥. Thus you wind up with 4♣ 5♣ J♦ 7♦ 4♥, Trip 4s with a Jack kicker. A possible winner, but test the waters with a raise. Anyone who raises back has at least Trips that would beat yours. Fold unless the raiser appears to be bluffing or clueless.

Strategy: Remember whatever cards you throw away. Speaking of which, almost always hold onto Aces and don't be the forgetful player who inevitably discards a 5! Watch for folks raising with abandon early. They're likely to have a high Pair or even Three of a Kind already. Finally, glean whatever info you can from players reacting to their hit-or-miss cards in the fourth round.

Options & Variations:
• Starting with the second round, have players turn up their kept cards for a more open, Stud-like game.

Pick 'Em

Piles, picking, and drawing.

Playing: Ante. Deal each player two cards. Deal three-card piles (one more than the number of players) face-down. Bet. The dealer flips every pile's top card. Starting to the dealer's left, each player in turn takes a pile into his hand. The unchosen pile is buried. Bet again. Each player may draw up to two cards. Then make a final bet.

The Reasoning Behind the Game: The freewheeling feeling of choosing a pile makes it all the more sweet or bitter when it does or doesn't work out. Of course, if the down cards are duds, they can both be replaced—with cards that also might not help.

Winning: Despite the smoke and mirrors, it's fairly close to Seven-Card Stud, which means that Two Pair wins frequently.

Example: In a six-person game, you're dealt 7♣ 8♥. It's your choice and the piles are topped with K♠ Q♦ 3♥ 9♦ 2♣ 3♠ and A♠. Grab the 9, since you have a good chance of getting a 5, 6, 10, or Jack underneath (giving you a Straight draw). If the hidden cards aren't high and don't help your Straight bid, then think about folding.

Strategy: Aggressive betting early indicates a strong hand—or a strong desire to pick the first pile, if playing the option below. Choose a pile based on pairing up, filling a Flush (if both hand cards are suited), building a Straight, or swiping a high card. Aggressive betting in the middle means a big hand if the player then draws none or one, but a bluff if they draw more! In the end, this can be a frustrating game of getting outguessed and outdrawn. Play tight.

Options & Variations:

• After the first bet, instead of defaulting to the player to the dealer's left, allow the player who made the last bet everyone called to take the first pile. Continue clockwise.

Pyramid (2)

Whereas "Pyramid (1)" (Section 4) centered on the shape's perimeter, this one builds upon its layers.

Playing: Ante. Deal each player four cards. Deal a three-row, six-card pyramid face-down. Bet. Flip a card from the base (of three). Bet. Flip another from the base. Bet. Flip the last base card. Bet. Flip a middle card. Bet. Flip the other middle card. Bet. Flip the apex. Bet again.

Forming the Hand: Players must use the top card, one from the middle two, one from the base, and two from their hand, making this game a close runner-up for Section 10 ("Wait...What Do I Have?").

The Reasoning Behind the Game: As the cards are revealed, players' hands are increasingly constrained.

Winning: Totally depends on what the board shows, but usually at least Trips.

3♠

4♣ J♦

6♥ 10♦ 9♣

Example: You're dealt 5♦ J♣ 4♥ 3♦. The very first card (the 6) gave you dozens of possible middle/top row Straight draws. Unfortunately, none of them happened. Your best hand uses the 10, Jack, and 3 to make Two Pair (Jacks and 3s). Given this pyramid, no Four of a Kind, Full House, or Flush is possible. A 2-5 or 5-7 in a player's hand could fill a Straight. A J-6, J-10, or J-9 could make a higher Two Pair. For Trips, a player would just need a Pair matching any of the pyramid's cards. In other words, if you have more than one opponent at this point, it'd be a good time to slip back into your sarcophagus.

Strategy: Before playing for real, deal yourself a pyramid and several four-card hands to practice figuring your hand versus the best possible hand. It'll make the process of running through all 36 possible hand combinations a little quicker at the table. And hopefully lead to less errors as well!

Options & Variations:

• In Finkel, it's a four-row, ten-card pyramid. The four-card base is turned up all at once, then the three-card row, then each in the two-card row, and finally the apex—each revelation followed by a bet. The hand must consist of the apex, one from the two-card row, one from either of the bottom two rows, and two from players' hands.

Do Ya?

Up to three chances for up card happiness.

Playing: Ante. Deal each player a down card (wild throughout their hand). Offer an up card to the player to the dealer's left. If refused, offer a second up card. If refused, deal the player the third up card (they're stuck with). Rotate the offer clockwise (with between zero and two cards). The next player can take one of the existing offer cards or see another, but must take the third one (if it comes to that). Each round ends by mucking any unwanted offer cards and betting. The process repeats until each player has five cards.

The Reasoning Behind the Game: Players see more cards and player decisions. Once a card is refused, the player can't use it.

Winning: Don't bother going for Straights or Flushes. Even a Full House is vulnerable. Probability dictates that if everyone stays in till the third up card, at least one of seven players is likely to pair up both their hole card and first up card. Since each player's hole card is wild, that means someone's likely to have Quads. So watch out for anyone with a Pair showing!

Example: You're dealt [4♣]. Your first offer is [7♣]. No reason to keep it, so you pass. Second offer is K♦. It's a good high card, so you take it. (The 7♣ is then offered to your neighbor.) The next offer that comes around to you is 4♥ Q♠. You grab the 4 so fast you almost rip it, giving you Three Kings and outing your hole card. (Your neighbor gets a chance at the Queen.) Your next offer comes 7♦, which you refuse. Second offer is 8♣. Time to take a step back and consider possible defensive plays. Any player with an Ace showing is a threat to your Kings. In this case, if an Ace-8 is showing, grab the 8 (in case it matches that player's hole card). Otherwise, ignore the 8 and hope for a King or 4 on the last card.

Strategy: Since most folks try to match up their wild hole card, make note of what cards players take. It might be a high (non-matching) or forced card. But by Third Street, at least one person will have matched up and it should be more obvious what each player wants.

Options & Variations:

- Each round, rotate the first card offer. (If you ever get lost, use the number of players' up cards as a guide. For instance, if everyone already has two up cards, the next first card offer starts three from the dealer.)
- Deal Auctioneer as Seven-Card Stud. Players pay 25, 50, and 75 cents respectively for each of the first three offer cards; and if they refuse all three, they have to pay $1 for a blind deck card. Offer card replacements automatically fill the most expensive slot.

Bid 'n' Buy (a.k.a. Bid 'Em)

If it strikes your fancy, it goes on the auction blocks!

Playing: Ante. Deal each player a down card. Offer the player to the dealer's left an up card. If interested in it, the player bids 25 cents for it. In turn, each other player verbally bids higher or passes on the card, until either a $2 max is reached or everyone without a card in the round has passed on it. (A player can't later bid on a card he has already passed on.) Either way, the last bidder pays the pot and gets the card. Offer the next person clockwise without a card in the round an up card. If not interested, the player must buy a blind deck card for 50 cents and the offer card moves left. The last player to get a card each round gets either the offer card for 25 cents or deck card for 50 cents. If there's a leftover card for the round, it's mucked. Either way, bet. Rotate the first right to bid/buy. Repeat the process until everyone has four up cards.

The Reasoning Behind the Game: Taking a blind card or offering everyone else the card you want is an interesting choice. One that gives an advantage to anyone in a later position. The third and fourth positions are ideal, since they get an early bid on the first offer cards and first crack at the final offer cards. As with other bidding games, this way of distributing cards considerably lengthens each hand. The buying, bidding, betting, and rotating can be hard to keep track of (that is why it is in this section).

Winning: The winners are all over the place. A high Pair could triumph among a series of busted hands. Or someone could manage to buy/luck into a Four of a Kind. It partly depends on how defensively people play. In the end, Two Pair is okay, but pay attention to the action each round.

Example: You've got [4♦] 6♠ 7♦ 8♣ with a chance to bid on the 10♠. The chances of getting a 5 from the deck aren't real good. Throw your $2 in the pot and grab the 10. Others will assume you have a 9 in the hole if you bet your fake Straight confidently. But you'll only be able to take it all the way against a couple of opponents, none of whom shows Trips or a possible Flush.

Strategy: Even if you think you might not get it, always bid if you're interested in a card. The deck card should be a last resort.

Options & Variations:
- Make Fifth Street a regularly dealt free card and offer an optional buy in the end.
- Try it as a Three-Card game (with a buy in the end).
- See other bidding-based games "Auction (1)" (Section 7), "Auction (2)" (Section 8), and "Auction Guts" (Section 12).

Nickel, Dime, Quarter (a.k.a. Free Enterprise, Grocery Store, Danny)

Stud meets Let's Make a Deal.

Playing: Ante. Deal each player two cards down. Deal three cards face-up in a row next to the deck and respectively designate them as costing 25, 50, and 75 cents. (Inflated from the olden days' nickel, dime, and quarter.) The player to the dealer's left can pay for any of the three or take a free one from the deck. When that player throws the proper money into the pot or requests the freebie, the dealer sends the appropriate card their way and replaces the up card (if necessary). After each player gets a card for the round, bet. At the beginning of the next round, replace a money card (if necessary)* and rotate the first right to purchase. Repeat the process until everyone has four up cards. Bet. Last card down. Bet.

The Reasoning Behind the Game: Players can either go free and random (per usual Stud) or pay and have a choice.

Winning: Look for Full Houses and near (if not) Perfect Lows.

Example: You've got [K♥ 10♥] 5♥ 8♦ 6♥ and the offer cards (in increasing value) are 2♣ 7♣ 7♥. You pay 75 cents for the 7♥, immediately signaling that you're not going Straight (or you would've taken the less expensive 7) and not thinking Low (or you would've taken the cheap Deuce). If any players have Two Pair or Trips showing, bet your made hand big. Or, if your game allows it, check and then raise. Either way, you want to get a sense of how strong everyone feels their hand is.

Strategy: As you're worrying about your own options, try to keep other players' decisions in mind as well. Not necessarily every player, but by Fifth Street you should have a pretty good idea of who is in direct competition with you. Try to be aware of their choices as best you can.

ACE OF SPADES	$ 2.50
JACK OF CLUBS	$ 14.50
DEUCE OF HEARTS	$ 4.75
ACE OF SPADES	$ 2.00
KING OF DIAMONDS	$ 6.75

The third money card is never replaced before the bet, since preemptively revealing it would give an unfair advantage to whomever is first to buy in the next round. If the last card taken in the round is a deck card, this isn't an issue.

Options & Variations:

- Wall Street adds a fourth ($1) card for purchase. When replacing an up card, slide the old ones and make the newest the most expensive.
- The Price Is Right offers 25, and 50-cent up cards or a 75-cent deck card dealt down.
- Abyssinia also uses two up cards and a deck card, but charges a preset price depending on the rank: 75 cents for an Ace, 25 cents for a 6 through 9, 50 cents for anything else.

Substitution (a.k.a. Replacement)

Pay to swap in better cards.

Playing: Ante. Deal each player three down and two up. Bet. Deal three cards face-up in a row next to the deck and designate them as costing 25, 50, and 75 cents; and a blind deck card $1. The player to the dealer's left may either stand pat or pay to exchange one of theirs for a money card. For a 25-, 50-, or 75-cent card, replace up cards up and down cards down (even though the money card was already seen), but for $1 deck cards always deal the replacement down. After each player gets a chance to swap cards for the round, bet. A second round of substitution. Final bet.

The Reasoning Behind the Game: Because upward of thirty up cards could show, dealing the deck cards down comes at a slight premium. In fact, they could potentially hide your hand completely. But that shouldn't automatically be your goal, since sometimes a little information inferred the wrong way can work better than giving no information at all!

Winning: As with "Nickel, Dime, Quarter," the Highs and Lows tend to be very good.

Example: You're dealt [2 ♠ 3♣ 5♦] J♥ 8♥. For your first substitution, you're offered 7♠ K♥ 10♣. Throw in 25 cents, grab the 7, and send the Jack packing. It gives you a half-decent Low and keeps players guessing whether you're actually going for a Straight. Of course, you can't make a Straight. But if an Ace, 4, or 6 is offered (with a preference toward the former) in the second round, you'll be able to forge a respectable Low (after substituting for the 8). By the way, as a general rule, you should bet at least to the level of your most recently purchased substitution card.

Strategy: Since the hands can get pretty good, don't go chasing Trips and Straights. Also, think first about replacing any heinous up cards with a down card from the deck as soon as possible. Assuming, of course, the very key card you need isn't just sitting there for the taking.

Options & Variations:

- With six or fewer players, deal two down and three up and add another substitution round.
- 2-5-10-20 (a.k.a. 2-5-10-Larry-Gary*) is initially dealt as Five-Card Stud. Following the Fifth Street bet, three substitution rounds begin. Starting with the high hand showing, players each stand pat or put $2** in chips in front of themselves. Once every player has financially indicated his intention to substitute or not, the action goes around again. This time, each player actually discards and gets a replacement. Play the $5 and $10 rounds similarly. A $20 card, if purchased, is an addition, not a substitution. In fact, a $20 card can be purchased and kept (always face-down) in any of the four buying rounds, not just the last. Strategically, this means it's most advantageous to buy the big one early and have six cards throughout. The game is generally played as High-Low with a declare.

Named for guys who bought $20 cards in every round and still lost (with nine cards)!

**Instead of these amounts, make it 50 cents, $1.25, $2.50, and $5 — or whatever amounts you want.*

Section 6 – Wild & Wacky

Completely untamed and kooky!

Anaconda (a.k.a. Pass the Trash)

Trading, rolling, and bluffing.

Playing: Ante. Deal each player seven cards. Bet. Players all pass three cards to their right (or whatever direction the dealer wants). Players muck the two cards they don't need and assemble their best five into the order in which they want to reveal them. Bet. Players roll their first card. Bet. Roll their second card. Bet. Third card. Bet. Fourth card. Bet. Declare. Bet* and reveal.

The Reasoning Behind the Game: The trading is mostly luck. But there's a science to properly revealing your hand. The goal is to represent the best hand you can while preserving the most mystery. Thus it's important to put the one key card you don't want players to see on the bottom of your face-down pile. For instance, the third of a kind in a Full House. It gives away your weaker rank and lowers your ability to effectively bluff, so hide it!

Winning: A decent Full House almost always wins High and the Lows tend to be 6s.

Example: You're dealt A♥ 4♠ 6♦ 7♠ 8♦ 9♣ 10♣. Pass the 8♦ 9♣ 10♣. (The Straight you had to break up wouldn't have won anyway.) You get 3♠ 4♣ 5♥ from your neighbor (who's apparently going High). One way to roll it would be exposing the A♥, 6♦, 3♠, then 4♣ (keeping the 5 hidden). As always, bet the Perfect Low like you have it. But bear in mind that you're vulnerable to a 6-5-4-2, 6-5-3, or actual 6-4.

Strategy: Remember what cards you give away. Also, process what the cards you're passed imply about that player's hand. Third, know when (someone else can know) you're beat. For instance, if you're holding 9♣ 9♦ 6♦ 6♥ 6♠ and someone with Q♠ Q♦ 10♠ 10♣ showing is betting into you, take a dive.

Options & Variations:

- When played with multiple trading rounds, pass three cards, two cards, and one card (each to a different person) and bet after each trade.
- Python deals five cards, has two passes (two cards and one card), and splits the pot between the players with the best three- and five-card High hands.

See the "Well I Do Declare" sidebar (Section 2) for several ending bet/declare options.

No Peeks (a.k.a. Showdown)

Out of sight, out of your mind.

Playing: Ante. Deal each player seven cards. Players may mix their cards, but can't look at them. (Ergo, the game's name.) The player to the dealer's left rolls one card and starts a bet. The next player to the left rolls cards until he beats that card* and starts a bet. It continues around, with each player flipping until they have the best hand showing** and then initiating a bet.

The Reasoning Behind the Game: Where you sit affects everything. In a later position, you might roll the rest of your cards to reveal a losing hand, whereas in an earlier position, you might roll only a couple of cards and torturously bet a hand for several rounds that only then turns out to be lousy.

Winning: Stay in with Three of a Kind or better.

Example: A player just made Three Jacks, you have 9♠ 7♠ 6♥ 8♠ K♠ 9♣ showing and it's your bet. Whether a call is smart depends on the ratio between the number of available 5s and 10s (to make your Straight) and the number of unseen cards. But also on how many other bets you'll need to call before you roll your last card and the strength of other players' hands. If the player with Trip Jacks is within two seats and it seems like a Straight could win, call the bet.

Strategy: What this game lacks in skill, it can make up for in drama. But don't let the hope of drama keep you in. You can still fold at any point and watch the drama unfold from a more comfortable, less expensive vantage point.

Options & Variations:

- In the "last game of the night" version, instead of betting, everyone just antes $2.
- The Limbo version deals players six cards and a seven-card ghost hand face-up to the table. As players roll their hands attempting to beat each other, if they beat the ghost hand's best five, they're out!
- Mexican Sweat deals a kill card face-up at the start. Anyone who rolls a matching card must fold.
- For more blind madness, see the "Midnight" version of "Baseball" just below.

    More cards don't necessarily outrank fewer. For instance, a Queen-6 doesn't beat a Queen. The player would need to roll a King, Ace, or Pair.

    **The "overburn" rule dictates that a player who rolls more than what's necessary to beat the board is fined. For instance, if the current best hand is a Pair of 6s and a player rolls a 7, 7, then 10, they pay the pot $2, since stopping at the Pair of 7s would've been sufficient. It keeps players alert and sustains the suspense.*

(Daytime, Basic, Little League) Baseball

Mixing America's two favorite pastimes.

Playing: All 3s and 9s are wild. If a 4 shows up, the player can buy an extra card for 50 cents. Other than that, it's played as regular Seven-Card Stud.

The Reasoning Behind the Game: The 3s refer to the number of strikes and outs. The 9s to the number of players and innings in a game. And the 4s to the number of bases and balls in a walk.

Winning: Four of a Kind will win, unless a Straight-Flush or Five of a Kind occurs.

Example: You end with [K♣ 3♦] 9♥ 4♠ 3♠ Q♣ 2♦ [Q♠]. Recapping the action: The 3 and 9 started you with Three Kings. The 4 on Fourth Street allowed you to buy what turned out to be the 3, giving you Four Kings. The Q♣ gave you a Royal Straight Flush (with the K♣ and three wilds). The 2 did nothing. Your final down card gave you Five Queens! It may seem obvious, but when you're focused on what you have during the game, it's easy to err. Something to be careful of, since some people play "what you call is what you have." Under that rule, if you'd mistakenly called the above hand as "Four Kings," a player with Four Aces could've beat you!

Strategy: If you don't at least have Trips by Fifth Street, consider folding. And in general, be aware of how many 3s, 9s, and 4s are out there.

Options & Variations:

- Establish if, when, and how players with 4s in the hole can purchase an extra card. When: Before dealing up cards the dealer asks around; before receiving an up card you request one; or never. How: Dealt up; dealt down as a courtesy; or dealt down for an extra fee.
- Instead of just seven, the Major League (a.k.a. Big League) version is played with nine innings (cards): Dealt three down, five up, one down. No extra cards for 4s.
- In the seasonal Winter League version, 4s (and their extra cards) and 9s are free. Players receiving a 3 up must match (part of) the pot, fold, or find someone else to match the pot and take the 3—possibly in trade for one of that player's other cards.
- The Midnight version is played in the style of "No Peeks" (described on page 68).
- Allow "The Natural"—the best hand with no wilds—to split the pot with the best overall hand.
- Name "strikes" or "rainouts." Certain cards that, when dealt up, immediately kill the hand. Either calling for a re-ante and re-deal, or just a new game altogether.

Stonehenge (a.k.a. Church, Iron Cross)

The trilithon of victory and the agony of defeat?

Playing: Ante. Deal each player three cards. Bet. Deal six community cards face-down in a four-card row with two pillar cards, mocking the famous Druid rock formation. Turn over each card and bet. (The corners are turned last.)

Forming the Hand: Players use the three in their hand plus any two consecutive community cards. The two corner cards are wild throughout.

The Reasoning Behind the Game: Everyone automatically has a wild card. Two, if a wild is repeated on the board (since it'd be consecutive with another wild).

Winning: Played High-only, Four of a Kind almost always wins. (A player need only pair up both a wild and non-wild board card.) At least two non-wild community cards 6 or less points to very good Lows.

Example: Even if you pair up none of the first four (non-wild) cards, it's not hopeless. Consider the figure on the left with a hand of 7♠ 3♦ 8♣. By combining the Jack-3 on the board with the double-wild 7-3 from your hand, you've got Four Jacks—definitely a contender!

7♦ 4♣ J♦ 3♥
6♥   10♦

Strategy: Adjust your eyes. It takes practice to see the hands correctly. For instance, looking closer at the example above, you'll notice you actually had a Straight-Flush (4♣ 7♦ 7♠ 3♦ 8♣)! By the way, a Five of a Kind (which would've beat your "improved" Straight-Flush) would've required a player to have Trip 6s, 4s, Jacks, or 10s; a pair of any of those with a wild; or a pair of wilds with any of those, making a loss possible, but not nearly likely enough to consider folding.

Options & Variations:
- No Holds Barred is a wrestling-themed cross between this and "Death Wheel" (Section 4). The "ring" has eight cards, three on each side. Players can use any from the four in their hand and any three consecutive ring cards. Since all four "turnbuckle" (corner) cards are wild, each player automatically has two wild cards.

Topsy Turvy (a.k.a. Honky Tonk)

A little help on the up-high and down-low.

Playing: Standard Five-Card Draw, but High-Low.

Forming the Hand: 3s are wild only in High hands; Kings are wild only in Low hands.

The Reasoning Behind the Game: It makes otherwise meaningless cards in either direction worth something.

Winning: High Trips is decent but vulnerable, since the 3s make filling Straights and Flushes easier. A 7-6 or better should win Low.

Example: You're dealt K♦ 3♣ A♥ 10♦ 6♠. For a split second you consider drawing to the (King-3) Pair of Cowboys. Then you sensibly go Low by tossing the 10. Picking up another 3, you now have K♦ 3♣ A♥ 3♥ 6♠, ruining your Low. But the Pair of Treys gives you Trip Aces! Definitely good enough to call with, although, if more than one player raises on the final bet (indicating a Straight or better), consider folding.

Strategy: You may need to get rid of a 3 or King sometime. For instance, you're dealt a K♣ 10♦ 10♠ 6♥ 4♣. You'd never pitch the Pair of 10s to draw two to a Low! The King could pair up High, but Two Pair isn't likely to win. You'd keep only the 10s and hope at least one of the three replacements is a 10 or 3 (a better than one in three chance).

Options & Variations:
- Howdy Doody applies the wild Kings/3s rule to "Anaconda" (earlier in this section).

Rollercoaster

A five-round Guts game alternating High and Low!

Playing: Ante 50 cents. Deal each player a card. A standard Guts drop. High card wins. Deal each player a second card. Drop. Low hand wins. Deal each player a third card. Drop. High hand wins. Deal each player a fourth card. Drop. Low wins. Final card, everyone's automatically in. High hand takes it.

The Reasoning Behind the Game: Each round, a sole player staying in wins the pot and everyone else re-antes. Otherwise, those who stay in compare cards; the best hand wins the pot; losers each replenish the pot with $2; and any droppers may re-ante or fold. (Folded players can't re-ante to get back in.) Comparing cards benefits only those who paid to stay in. But conversely, the $2 fixed penalties for staying in and losing can really add up over five rounds!

Winning: With six players, the winning hands might be:

Round 1: Queen
Round 2: 6 Low
Round 3: A moderate Pair to Flush
Round 4: 8 Low
Round 5: A high Pair to Two Pair

Example: Consider the unlikely-but-ultimate hand, A♥ 2♥ 3♥ 4♥ 5♥. First round, Ace-high. Second round, at least a 5 Low. Third round, either a Flush or Straight Flush. Fourth round, at least a 5 Low. And fifth round a Straight-Flush. Not too many other hands could potentially win this many rounds. But it's still fun to dream about!

Strategy: Play each round separately. Don't let how much you won or lost in the last round affect your play. Also, use the opportunity to see others' cards to your advantage.

Options & Variations:

- Double the initial ante to juice the pot. After the first round, either go back to a normal ante or leave it high.
- If everyone drops, everyone pays the fixed limit penalty.
- Instead of fixed penalties, with pot matching this could quickly get out of hand!
- See "3-5-7" (Section 10) for a slightly more refined brand of wackiness.

Jack the Shifter

Changing the game midstream.

Playing: Dealt as regular Seven-Card Stud, until a Jack appears up. Whoever got the Jack can name any other appropriate Stud game. What's named is what the game changes to, until the next Jack appears.

Reasoning: The new game called has to be a standard game format ("Baseball," "Pass a Card, Buy a Card," etc.). In other words, a player can't simply call "Seven-Card Stud, 8s and 4s are wild" or "All Clubs are wild" based on what cards they have.

Winning: Players will stare at their cards to double-check what they have!

Example: On Fifth Street, you have [2 ♠ 10♦] 2♥ 10♣ J♥. What's the perfect game to call right now? Either "Kankakee" (Section 2) or "Low Card in the Hole" (Section 10) would make your 2s wild, giving you Four 10s—at least until the next Jack... ("Low Chicago" would've made sense too, if you only wanted half the pot.)

Strategy: Look for key cards such as Spades ("Chicago") or 3s and 9s ("Baseball"). In the absence of anything that could give you a winning hand, just call whatever's fun.

Options & Variations:
• A Jack on the last up card neutralizes the game back to regular Seven-Card Stud.
• To avoid mass confusion, Jacks in the hole should probably be ignored.

Section 7 – Match Games

Focused on the phenomena of like ranks and suits.

Bing-Bang-Bong

Un-neighborly matching.

Playing: Players place three piles each totaling $2 in front of themselves. Deal each player seven cards. The player to the dealer's left flips a card. The player to his left flips a card. And so on. If during the sequence a player matches a card just flipped, the player to his right pushes one of his piles into the pot—two piles, if it's the third in a row; all their piles, if it's the fourth. The action is continuous, without betting.

The Reasoning Behind the Game: Later positions have a slight advantage. Counting cards is possible—but the dealer may make it slightly tougher by asking players to turn their non-matched discards face-down. If necessary, shuffle the discards and re-deal.

Winning: The last player with at least one pile wins.

Example: You're left with 4♣ 4♦ Q♥. Playing the odds, you lay down a 4—only to see it matched! You lose a pile. But the next player plays another 4 and the player to your left loses his last two piles! Not only does that mean less competition, but also that playing your other 4 next time is perfectly safe.

Strategy: From most to least ideal, you want to play from: Quads; a Pair already matched; a single card already matched; any card just played; a random card. As simple as it is, this game still requires steady attention.

Options & Variations:
- Loudly shout "Bing!" or "Bing-Bang!" or "Bing-Bang-Bong!" in your neighbor's ear when you match them (if you don't mind a beating).

Match It (a.k.a. Murder (2))

Matching up cards could be bad. Deadly bad.

Playing: Separate from the regular betting, if during Seven-Card Stud anyone pairs their up cards, they have to either fold or match the pot—thus making "Match It" a delicious double-entendre!

The Reasoning Behind the Game: A penalty for good hands?

Winning: Although Straights and Flushes may seem more effi-cient (since they don't contain a Pair and won't force a pot match), Two Pair is a more frequent winner.

Example: On Sixth Street against three opponents, you've got [8♠ J♥] 2♣ A♠ 10♠ 2♠. Between the Spades, Aces, Jacks, and 10s, you figure fourteen cards could help you. But to match the pot now against three other players would require a monster hand (of the Full House caliber). Otherwise you're simply feeding the pot with no promise of any return. Bad investment. Fold!

Strategy: Don't match the pot before Fifth Street if the matching Pair is 7s or less (unless you have hidden cards complementing the Pair). And from Fifth Street on—especially since it may have already been matched—don't match the pot unless you have Two Pair. Speaking of which, in the off chance you pair your up cards a second time in the same hand, don't match the pot unless you've already made the Full House!

Options & Variations:

- If no folding or pot matching occurs, re-deal the hand until one of the two happens.
- Real masochists deal it two down, five up—or one down, six up!
- Make matching hole and up cards both wild—doubly nice, since a good hand is assured and no (pot) matching is necessary!
- See the "Dirty Schultz" variation of "Follow the Queen" in Section 10.

Stockbridge

Matching ranks and suits determine the widow.

Playing: Ante. Deal each player five. Deal the board two overlapping "control" cards, followed by three "subject" cards in a row (all face-down), next to which the deck is placed. Bet. Flip both control cards. Bet. Flip the first subject card. Bet. The second subject card. Bet. The third subject card. Bet. Flip the fourth subject card (on top of the deck). Bet. In High-Low, there's a declare and final bet.

Forming the Hand: Each of the subject cards must match either the suit or rank of one of the control cards, or it's banished from the widow. Figure the best five between the five in your hand, the two control cards and the zero to four subject cards.

The Reasoning Behind the Game: Consider these control card combos: 10♠ 7♣, 10♠ 10♦, 10♠ 2♠. They respectively allow twenty-eight, twenty-four, and seventeen subject cards to stay in the widow. The potential for good hands becomes exponentially better with more (related) common cards.

Winning: With only suit matches, expect Flushes. If the widow pairs up, expect at least a Full House. The Lows aren't affected much by the matching dynamic, but they're obviously better with two or more low cards in the widow.

Example: You're dealt 10♣ 8♠ K♠ Q♠ 6♠. The 10♠ gave you a Flush right away, so you bet strong. The K♥, not being a 10, 7, Spade, or Club, didn't stay. The matching 7♦ made it likely that a Flush wouldn't win. The 9♠ was fairly meaningless. But the 10♥ gave you a nice Full House. Although, you'll have to split your winnings with the owner of the 10♦, assuming no one holds both the other 7s or a pat hand with a higher Full House or better.

10♠ 7♣
(K♥) 7♦ 9♠ 10♥

Strategy: If your starting five doesn't have a Pair, Flush draw or three to a good Low, it could be a long and costly hand for you. Remember, after the control cards flop, you've already got seven cards to make a hand. So don't rest your hopes and dreams on a particular other card coming up. It may, but the times it doesn't will be more frequent — and expensive.

Options & Variations:
- In Red and Black, deal each player four cards and set the widow with two four-card columns (designated "Red" and "Black"). Each round, flip a card in each column. If the card's color is appropriate to the column it's in, it stays. After the fourth round, players make their best five from all the cards in their hands and those remaining in both columns.

Auction (1)

Matching doesn't bid well...

Playing: Ante. Deal each player five cards and set the widow with three cards in the top row, three in the middle, and two on the bottom. Bet. Flip the first card in the top row. Each player, starting with the player to the dealer's left, may verbally bid (at least 25 cents, with 25-cent increments) or pass on the card. When a $2 max is reached or the passes go once around, the last player to bid puts money in the pot and gets the auction card. Bet. Flip and bid on each of the other two cards in the top row and bet. Flip the first card in the middle row. Discard all matching cards (by rank) on top of it. Bet. Flip and discard onto each of the other two cards in the middle row and bet. Flip the first card of the bottom row. This is a common card. Bet. Flip the last card, also common. Final bet. (Rotate the bidding and betting each round.)

Forming the Hand: Your best five from any of what's left in your hand plus the two common cards.

The Reasoning Behind the Game: The auction row allows folks to pay to improve. The second row can be deadly—especially for those with Pairs or Trips! And the last row gives a couple of freebies. In the end, players will have seen 1/4 of the deck and could theoretically have as many as ten cards or as few as two.

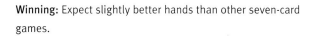

Winning: Expect slightly better hands than other seven-card games.

Example: You're dealt J♣ J♥ 5♦ 5 ♣ 8♠. First chance you had, you bid $2 to get the Jack, giving you a Full House! The 9 and 7 did nothing for you. The Queen didn't affect you. But the fourth Jack showed up in

J♠ 9♣ 7♦

Q♦ J♦ 3♠

5♠ 5♥

the second row—you had to discard both your Jacks, leaving you a lousy Pair of 5s! Heart-broken, you stayed in anyway. The 3 didn't affect you. The first 5 in the bottom row gave you Trips. The last card was the case 5, giving you Quads—from amazing to depressing, back to amazing, all in the same hand!*

Strategy: Be wary of any auction cards that wind up matching a common card. And in general, how many cards each player has. Consider the effect of the cards discarded. If 10's are discarded, you know that a 9-high Straight is the best possible. Straights are very vulnerable hands in this game! Finally, watch out for players who don't bid, don't discard, and keep betting. They're either completely lost or have a pat hand!

Options & Variations:

- Pyramid (3) offers nine cards of multi-row action. The top two cards indicate what's wild (but aren't common); the middle three are community cards; and the bottom four are the "discard if you match" cards.
- See other bidding-based games "Bid 'n' Buy" (Section 5), "Auction (2)" (Section 8), and "Auction Guts" (Section 12).
- Also, see Section 11 ("Fundraisers").

*As farfetched as it sounds, this actually happened to/for my dad's poker buddy, Ed. In the real story, however, he folded after losing the Jacks. His doctors have recently upgraded his condition to "fairly stable."

Numbers (a.k.a. Blackout)

Lose everything to win?

Playing: Ante. Deal each player five cards. Deal a row of seven cards in the center. Each round, flip one of the center cards. Players discard any of like rank and bet. (Rotate the starting bet each round.)

The Reasoning Behind the Game: If a board card repeats, it's ignored and replaced with one from the deck that doesn't match another one.

Winning: The first player to lose all his cards wins. If no one loses all his cards, declare and bet. Split the pot between the players with the highest and lowest point totals, according to the card values in

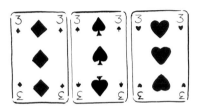

"Blackjack" (Section 11). If at least four piles rank 7 or higher, decent Highs are around 30 and safe Lows are under 10. If the majority of piles rank 7 or lower, the Highs are more around 40 and the Lows just over 10. (Kind of sounds like a weather report!)

Example: With four Aces, it'd be possible to declare "Both," since the hand's worth 4 or 44—both potential winners. Of course, the tricky part would be getting dealt four Aces!

Strategy: Only the last two bets (before and after the declare) really mean anything. Since people inevitably equate others' totals with the number of cards they hold, it might be possible to bluff. Low with a single high card or High with multiple Low cards. Even though neither hand would likely win in an actual showdown.

Options & Variations:
- Figure out a way to deal with ties, such as turning additional deck cards until a player matches one (and wins).
- The 333 version deals three cards to each player and four to the board. If no one loses all his cards, the closest totals to three and thirty-three split the pot (after a declare).

Section 8 – Simply Insane

Above and beyond the normal nonsensical home games dreamt up.

Auction (2)

Bidding on every up card?

Playing: Deal each player two down cards. For the up cards, do one of the following:

1. Each round, deal enough cards for everyone face-up in the middle. Players bid for the right to choose by secretly putting up to $2 in chips in their hands under the table and revealing them on the dealer's command. The player offering the most (as their "bid") can choose whichever card he wants. The next highest bidder chooses second, and so on. If players bid the same amount, the one in earlier position gets the honor.
2. Flip one card. The player to the dealer's left verbally bids or passes on it (at least 25 cents with 25-cent increments). The bids and passes go around the table until someone bids the $2 max or everyone passes. Either way, whoever bid last pays the pot and gets the card. Flip another card. The next player clockwise without a card bids first on it.

Once everyone has a card for the round, bet. Repeat until each player has four up cards. Deal each player a down card and bet.

The Reasoning Behind the Game: The chips-under-the-table method is operationally clunky. The one-card-at-a-time method is like "Bid 'n' Buy" (Section 5), but without the simple buy-out option. Both methods are tedious and give an advantage to those in middle position.

Winning: Any hand a player openly buys will tend to be better. Don't stay in High with less than Trips or Low with higher than a 7-4.

Example: You've got [6♦ 7♠] 5♠ 9♥ and the round's auction cards are A♥ K♠ J♥ J♠ 8♠ 4♣ 2♦. Unless another player has a similar Straight draw, your desired card (the 8) won't be coveted by other players. Especially with the other good high and low cards offered. Using either method, bid a minimal 25 cents and see where it takes you.

Strategy: Invariably in auction games like this, players bid even when they don't want a card, just to drive up the price for others. Get in the habit of doing this every so often. It gets other players not knowing if you really want a card when you bid on it. If players believe it's just another ploy of yours, they may be less likely to bid. And you could wind up with a bargain.

Options & Variations:
- Since Five-Card Stud also has four up card rounds, it'll take about as long.
- Take away both the regular betting and the cap on the bidding.
- See "Auction (1)" (Section 7) and "Auction Guts" (Section 12).

Blind Stud

"No Peeks" until the end?

Playing: Deal three down. Bet. Deal one down. Bet. Another down. Bet. Yet another down. Bet. Final down card and bet.

The Reasoning Behind the Game: There's no reasoning to be had. This game is pure madness!

Winning: This game has no winners. But Two Pair might take the pot.

Example: You're dealt [X X X X X X X]. You wind up with 8♦ 6♠ 7♠ 5♥ 3♣ Q♥ A♦. You bet along the way. You lost.

Strategy: Seriously, why are you even reading this part?

Options & Variations:
• Just have everyone put a few bucks in the pot and deal them all face-up.
• Be completely absurd and play it High-Low with a declare!

Buddha's Folly (a.k.a. Circle Jerk)

Paradoxical passing and Guts?

Playing: Ante. Deal each player five cards. Deal an extra one to the player to the dealer's left, who discards and passes one to his left. The discarding and passing continues until the same card's passed all the way around the table. After a Guts-styled drop, if one player stays in, he wins the pot. If multiple players stay in, they compare hands and each loser pays the pot $2. Collect, shuffle, and re-deal the cards, rotating the player receiving the extra card. Play until someone wins the pot.

The Reasoning Behind the Game: After all the passing and hand improvement, it seems unlikely that only one player would stay in for the drop. But it does happen. Especially a few rounds in, when certain players have gained a deeper understanding of how "All life is suffering."

Winning: Almost everyone goes for a Full House. The only questions are whether you'll get yours and whether it'll be good enough to win.

Example: You're dealt 10♥ J♠ Q♦ 9♠ 5♠. The 8♠ comes. A Straight won't win, but it doesn't hurt. Next time around (with 10♥ J♠ Q♦ 9♠ 8♠) you get the 8♦ and say goodbye to the 9. The 5♥ comes next and you reject it. With 10♥ J♠ Q♦ 8♦ 8♠, the 10♣ is passed to you. Taking it gives you 10s and 8s with a Queen kicker. People seem to be doing more passing than discarding. Hold out as long as you can for a 10 or 8. If by the end, you haven't made your Boat, drop.

Strategy: Early on, accept only cards that help your hand. Toward the middle hoard low cards. People might pass enough low cards for you to build a Full House. And if not, they're still a great placeholder. Later, when you finally get your key card, you'll want to pass the worst possible card so that it comes all the way back around to you!

Options & Variations:
- Make the passed cards face-up.
- Play it as single-round Guts: The losers who stay in each pay $1 to the pot, which is then collected by the player who stayed in with the best hand, ending the game.

- Trees (a.k.a. Trading Spaces) swaps cards in more of a free-for-all. After the initial ante, five cards, and bet, players openly and simultaneously trade the same number of cards with each other. When no one wishes to trade anymore, a final bet and the best hand—probably Quads—wins.

Give 'n' Take (a.k.a. Put 'n' Take)

Simply nerve-wracking credit and debit?

Playing: Deal each player five cards. The dealer flips one of his own. Players all flip one of theirs and put 25 cents into the pot for each matching card, which they discard face-up onto the dealer's. The dealer flips a second card. This time, players put 50 cents in for matches, which they also discard. The action is similar for the next three rounds, with the price per card doubling to $1, $2, and $4. Once the dealer's hand is fully exposed, all the matching cards are mucked and the dealer deals himself another five face-down. The other players continue to play their original hands from the "Give" rounds. Now starts the "Take" rounds, in which they take out 25 cents, 50 cents, $1, $2, and $4 from the pot for matching each of the dealer's cards.

The Reasoning Behind the Game: In the first round, matching the dealer's cards with the players' is key (to maximize the pot-inflation). In the second, matching the dealer's cards to his own is key (to minimize the pot-draining). For instance, if the dealer's second hand contains two 9's, players will have to ditch their 9's on the first, less expensive one and won't have any when the higher denomination shows.

Winning: If at the end there's a surplus in the pot, the dealer keeps it. If the pot doesn't provide enough to properly pay the other players, the dealer has to delve into his own chips to do so.

Example: Round one, the dealer has 4♦ 7♣ J♠ 10♥ 4♥. Players toss in no 4s (+0 cents), one 7 (+50 cents), three Jacks (+$3), two 10s (+$4), and no 4s (+$0), totaling +$7.50. Round two, the dealer gets 5♠ 6♣ 8♥ 3♣ Q♠. Players toss in one 5 (-25 cents), no 6s (-0 cents), two 8s (-$2), one 3 (-$2), and two Queens (-$8), totaling -$12.25. Thus the dealer loses $4.75. Could've been worse!

Strategy: The best time to call this game is when you have a bunch of extra chips clogging up your area of the table. That is, it's a good, unskilled way to lose money!

Options & Variations:
• Vary the amounts put in and taken out.

Hurricane

Two-Card Stud?

Playing: Ante. Deal each player one down. Bet (started by player to dealer's left). Deal each player one up. Bet (started by player showing high card). Show them.

Forming the Hand: Straight Poker. Best Pair or highest cards win.

The Reasoning Behind the Game: When three is too many cards and Guts seems scary?

Winning: Again, a Pair, Ace, and/or both cards 10 or higher will win.

Example: You're dealt [3♣] 9♠. You're not going to win. Unless... Perhaps if you bet big enough, folks'll think you have an Ace or another 9 under there. A bluff that could work, assuming no one has a Pair of 10s or higher.

Strategy: If someone showing a 7 or lower is staying in, they either have a matching card or Ace in the hole. If you can't beat that, fold.

Options & Variations:

- Frustration is the Draw version, in which players can exchange up to two.
- The High-Low version features a declare and third bet.

Pick a Partner

Combining forces to win in tandem?

Playing: Ante. Deal each player five cards. Bet. Roll a card. The player showing the highest card (in the earliest position, if there's a tie) chooses a partner. The unpartnered player with the next highest card picks someone. And so on, until everyone has a partner. (Hopefully there's an even number of players.) Each set of partners merges their unrolled hands. From those eight, each partner extracts three and they muck the extra two. Bet. Roll a card. Bet. Roll a card. Bet. Roll the last.

Forming the Hand: Each player is going for his best Monte Carlo hand.

The Reasoning Behind the Game: Instead of dealing with all the combining and splitting up, it seems more logical to simply call "Four-Card Three-Card" (Section 11).

Winning: Whichever partnership includes the High hand splits the pot between the partners. Unless one of the partners folds, in which case the one staying in with the High hand gets it all. It'll be Three of a Kind or a Straight-Flush.

Example: You're dealt 10♠ 10♣ 9♣ 4♣ K♦. The King's the oddball, so you display it as your mating call. You wind up first to choose and, for some inexplicable reason, go with someone else displaying a Diamond. Your partner's unrolled hand is K♥ 10♥ A♦ 5♣. That third 10 will help make a decent contender for best hand. You let your partner have the 4♣ 5♣ 9♣. Just a Flush, but it'll look like a Straight-Flush when rolled right, hopefully making the other sets of partners shake in their collective sets of boots.

Strategy: Once partnered, don't worry about trying to make two hands...that might both lose. Focus on forging one really great contender, unless you want to screw your partner. But that's your business.

Options & Variations:

- Henway deals each player ten cards, which they split into two hands, roll and declare a la "Anaconda" (Section 6).
- Ten-Card Regrets is a blind—or at least nearsighted—version of "Henway." The pile of ten cards is divided one per round. Players flip and quickly place a card in either their "High" or "Low" hand, then bet. In the end, each hand must wind up with five. The cards speak and the winners split the pot.

Rotation

Stud with a twist?

Playing: The dealer names a rank as the game's "rotation card." For each rotation card dealt during a round of up cards, rotate all that round's cards one player to the left.

The Reasoning Behind the Game: This "involuntary pass a card" rule doesn't necessarily help or hurt anyone, but does add interesting antics to the mix.

Winning: With no additional conscious decisions, winning hands should be the same as regular Stud.

Example: The rotation card called is 4. You're dealt [4♣ 4♦] Q♥. Predictably, the next couple of rounds are boring. On Sixth Street, with [4♣ 4♦] Q♥ 3♦ 2♠ you're dealt the 4♠. You're frustrated knowing you're about to lose your Triplets to the rotation until you see that the player two to your right just got the 4♥. After some quick math, you figure out that with the double-rotation it'll get passed to you! Thus you've made your Trips and bet them strong. Two players drop. A player or two with Two Pair bet into you. You raise right back. Since the last card is down, no more rotations. It's just all about Seventh Street.

Strategy: As with other gimmicky games, do your best not to be distracted. Sit back and play regular Stud the best you know how. If cards shift, they shift.

Options & Variations

• Make the rotation card wild, to the instant delight of the player to your left.
• Choose two rotation cards, one going left and one going right, affecting play either way or canceling out each other.
• In Twister, any player dealt an 8 up can call "Twister!" Each player must give the the dealer three of his cards. Shuffle the cards caught in the twister and redistribute them (up and down, if necessary).

SECTION 9 – Casino Cousins

"This Ain't Vegas"

Certain adjustments have been made to these popular casino games, primarily because the home dynamic is one where every player is an active participant with a stake in the game. Also, since the players deal instead of paid employees for a casino with seemingly unlimited resources, there are no vigs, progressives, or bonus payouts for great hands. Other than that, these slightly altered commercial favorites are about the same.

Adapted from the world of glitter to fit neatly into your dining room.

Pai Gow Poker

Battling dual hands.

Playing: Ante $2. Each player is dealt seven cards and splits them into a five-card hand and two-card hand. Bet. Reveal the two-card hands. Bet. Reveal the five-card hands. The players with the best of each sized hand split the pot.

Forming the Hand: Each player's five-card hand must be better than his two-card hand. In other words, an Ace in the two-card hand means the five-card hand must contain at least a Pair. A Pair in the two-card hand means the five-card hand must contain at least a better Pair.

The Reasoning Behind the Game: Without the rule on splitting hands, players would unfairly stack their two-card hands to steal half the pot.

Winning: The five-card winner might be Two Pair or a high Pair and a kicker. And the two-card winner will be a Pair or Ace-high most of the time. If the two-card hands tie, the player with the better five-card hand wins. (And vice versa, in the unlikely case of identical five-card hands.)

Example: You're dealt A♣ A♥ J♠ 10♦ 8♣ 7♥ 2♠. The Aces may not win in the five-card hand. And Jack-10 is unlikely to do it in the two-card hand. But you might finagle half the pot by splitting the hand A♣ J♠ 8♣ 7♥ 2♠ and A♥ 10♦. The Ace-Jack better than the Ace-10 makes it legal!

Strategy: Double-check first for Straights or Flushes (since those are strong) in the five-card hand, even if it leaves you with a lousy two-card hand. Otherwise, make the best two-card hand you can. For instance, with a Pai Gow (only High Card), keep the high card in the five and use your second and third highest for the two. It's your best move and might actually make you a contender with the little hand.

Options & Variations:

- Add a "bug" (Joker) to the deck. It isn't wild per se, but can be used as an Ace or to fill a Straight or Flush. Whichever helps the hand more.
- Rather than all at once, deal three, two, and two, or two, two, two, and one, etc. to add more suspense and betting.
- Play with a declare (one chip to win the two-card hand, two for the five-card, or three for both), followed by a full reveal, rather than in two stages.
- Play until a single player wins with the best of both hands.

Let It Ride

Fling a fixed bet or fold.

Playing: Ante $1. Players place three piles each totaling $1 in front of themselves. Deal each player three cards and two to the board. Players either push one of their stacks into the pot or fold (and take back the rest of their chips). Flip the first board card. The remaining players either push another stack or fold. Flip the other board card. Players riding it out shove in their last stack and compare hands.

The Reasoning Behind the Game: Fixed betting takes away the guesswork. Seeing the first three cards gives an opportunity to fold any awful hands. The community cards limit how good the hands can be.

Winning: A high Pair wins much of the time. Always ride out Two Pair or better.

Example: You're dealt Q♦ 8♣ 5♠. Following the advice given below, you fold. The first community card is the Q♠. You curse the idiot who wrote the advice below (under your breath, so as not to give away anything). The second community card is the A♦. Two players stay in. A player with 10s loses to a player with a Pair of Aces. You saved a couple of bucks. I accept your apology.

Strategy: Don't let your money ride without a Pair, three to a Straight or Flush, and/or two cards 10 or higher in your starting three. Get off the ride if the first community card doesn't help you and you're not paired up. Finally, end the ride if your best five isn't at least a high Pair with a kicker. It may be tough to fold, but these rules will make sure you don't get taken for a ride over the long haul.

Options & Variations:
• See the "Three Plus Two" version of "3-5-7" in Section 10.

Caribbean Stud

All hands on the deck!

Playing: Ante. Deal each player five cards down, plus four down and one up to the board. Bet. Flip two more board cards. Bet. Flip the last two board cards. Anyone who can't beat the board hand must fold. Everyone else bets. Players compare hands.

The Reasoning Behind the Game: Revealing the board in stages allows weak players to fold and strong players to build up the pot. And qualifying the hands raises the quality of the winning hand. To the chagrin of those who stayed in and didn't make the cut!

Winning: As in "No Draw" (Section 3), the hands tend to be modest. Any Pair has a shot, but especially 10s or better.

Example: You're dealt 6♠ 7♠ 8♥ 9♠ J♠. Should you go for the Straight or the Flush? Actually, since it's not a Draw game, you can't "go for" either! In fact, as with about half the hands dealt, you should fold.

Strategy: If you have anything better than a Pair, bet it from the start. Consider if you were dealt Trips and the board turned up Two Pair. It might disqualify the two or three other players still in, leaving you, the lone player, to collect a relatively thin pot. So don't wait for the third bet. It may not happen!

Options & Variations:

- If no one beats the board, collect, reshuffle, and re-deal the cards. Players who folded may re-ante to rejoin the action. Continue until at least one player beats the board.
- Play with fixed bets, like "Let It Ride" (just above).
- See "Beat the Deck," described in "Additional Guts Games & Rules" (Section 12).
- Also see casino games "Blackjack" (a.k.a. "21") and "Between the Sheets" (a.k.a. "Red Dog") in Section 11.

SECTION 10 – Wait...What Do I Have?

Voted "Most Likely to Befuddle" by a panel of confused experts.

Low* Card in the Hole (a.k.a. Shipwreck)

Know when to hole 'em.

It's crucial to establish whether Aces are just high, just low, or both!

Playing: Initially dealt as regular Seven-Card Stud. Each player's lowest down card is wild throughout his hand. Each player requests his last card up or down.

The Reasoning Behind the Game: Everyone automatically has at least one wild card. Players opt to have their last card up if they fear a down card might adversely affect their hand.

Winning: It'll take Quads.

Example: With [6♣ 6♦] K♦ 9♠ 10♠ 3♠, you're deciding how to get your last card. If the card's a King, 9, or 10 (up or down), you'll have made a decent Four of a Kind. If it's a 3 down, you'll have made Four 6s. A 3 up (or 6 either way) would give you Four 3s. Everything else leaves you with a lousy Three Kings or pitiful Kings and 6s. Take from this confusion that you may not have a great shot at winning, but it seems like down's a better way to go.

Strategy: As you look around at everyone's up cards...

Notice	Because
Who's got low cards showing	They're more likely to match their hidden cards.
Who's paired up	It's that much closer to a winning hand.
Who's got any of your low cards showing	It decreases your chance to make a winning hand.

Any of the above is bad for you. Since Four of a Kind is likely to win, you'll have to pair up somewhere. If you haven't done so by Fifth Street and don't have a Straight-Flush draw, seriously consider folding.

Options & Variations:

- Despite revealing information about players' hands, charge extra to get Seventh Street up (since it's a privilege to avoid possibly changing one's hand).
- Maximize the intrigue of this feature by combining it with "Roll Your Own" (Section 2).
- In the "Cincinnati"-like Lame-Brain Pete, the lowest of the four widow cards is wild in everyone's hands.

Follow the Queen (a.k.a. Chase the Lady)

All hail her highness.

Playing: Dealt as regular Seven-Card Stud. If a Queen appears up, the next card dealt up (even at the start of a new round) is wild. If another Queen is later dealt up, that next card is the only wild. If a Queen is the last card dealt up, nothing's wild.

The Reasoning Behind the Game: The fickle Fates decide what's wild—which can be tricky to keep track of!

Winning: Three of a Kind is respectable, but a Straight wins more often when something's wild.

Example: You're dealt [3♣ 6♠] 10♦ 6♣ 4♥ 7♣ [2♣]. The 6♣ followed a Queen, giving you Trip 10s on Fourth Street. Another Queen showed up the very next round, followed by a 7 that killed your Trips. Until Sixth Street, when that wild 7 gave you Trip 6s. No more Queens appeared, leaving 7s wild. The 2 down didn't seem like much—until you realized that it filled a Straight! Not a high one, but definitely worth betting.

Strategy: If your good hand is based on a wild card, don't bet the farm until after Sixth Street. Things could easily change before then!

Options & Variations:

- Make the Queens themselves wild—either throughout or just when dealt down.
- Dirty Gerty (a.k.a. Dirty Lizzie or Black Mariah (1)) dictates that if the Queen of Spades appears up, it

resets the hand. Immediately stop, re-ante and re-deal the hand until Ole Lady Spade doesn't show up.
- Make no Queens showing up reset the hand.
- In Dirty Schultz (a.k.a. Change the Diaper), when a player pairs his up cards, the next card dealt up is wild for everyone. Alternatively, if a card dealt up matches any existing up card, the next one could be wild. But that makes for a head-spinning array of changes throughout the average deal.

Twin Beds

You've dealt your bed, now lie in it.

Playing: Ante. Deal each player four cards. Deal ten cards to the board in two rows of five. Bet. Each round, flip two cards and bet. (As usual, rotate the starting bettor each round.) When all ten are face-up, declare High-Low and bet.

Forming the Hand: Your best five of the four in your hand plus either row of five.

The Reasoning Behind the Game: With two different nine-card options, it can take the players a while to figure out all of their possibilities.

Winning: Expect the Lows to be excellent. The High will likely be a Full House (if the board pairs) or Flush.

Example: You're dealt 10♣ 2♠ 5♦ J♥. As the board shown here was revealed column by column... The A♦/9♦ gave you ideas of a Low up top and high Straight on bottom. The top row pairing Aces and you pairing 2s didn't help either cause. The 5♥ seemed like a good thing. But then the Jack gave you three Pair, the best two of which were the Aces and Jacks. The 5♠/6♣ was the most confusing. Instead of making a Low on bottom, you pulled a low

A♦ A♥ 5♥ J♠ 5♠
9♦ 2♣ 3♠ 4♣ 6♣

Straight. Completely overshadowed by both Full Houses (5s Full of Jacks and 5s Full of Aces) up top. Unfortunately, all someone would need is a single Ace in his hand to go both ways—Aces Full up top and the Perfect Low on bottom—and you don't have one.

Strategy: Given the number of cards, someone likely has the best possible hand. In the example above, a player with an Ace had an unbeatable Low. And the only thing that could've beat the Aces Full would've been if that same player had the fourth Ace!

Options & Variations:

- Pharaoh uses the same setup, but requires that players use exactly two from their hand and exactly three from either row. Recycling the above example, your best hand (5s Full of Jacks) would've actually been slightly stronger.
- The similar Nud-Nick uses the same board, but deals players five cards and requires that they either stand pat; use two from their hand and three from one row; or three from their hand plus any column of two.
- Sidecars travels even further down the causeway of complexity. Deal players four cards down and one up. High card bets. Each round, reveal a column of Xs and bet. Reveal each O separately and bet. Players form their hands with an X from each row, an O and two from their hand. If this game isn't appropriate for this section, nothing is!

```
X X X X
O           O
X X X X
```

Omaha (Hold 'Em)

More cards, flexibility, and restrictions than Texas.

Playing: Deal each player four cards. The betting, widow, and revelation are identical to "Texas Hold 'Em" (Section 4).

Forming the Hand: Your best five must be composed of exactly two from your hand and exactly three from the field. When played High-Low, there's often an 8 qualifier Low.

The Reasoning Behind the Game: Since after the Flop every player already has six possible five-card hands, someone often has the best hand possible. Very different from Texas! The implication of an 8 qualifier is that for a Low to happen, at least three cards from the field must be an 8 or lower. Otherwise, it's one winner, High only. Or at the dealer's prerogative, it can be declared High-only from the start.

Winning: A Straight, Flush, or Full House is statistically likely when three to a Straight, three to a Flush or at least a Pair show in the widow. If a Low is possible, the best or second-best possible one usually wins.

Example: You were dealt 6♣ 7♣ 8♣ 8♥. The widow wound up 4♦ 5♣ 9♣ J♦ K♦. You bet like a demon after the 4♦ 5♣ 9♣ flopped. Wait. Did you have a Straight...a Flush...a Straight-Flush? Nope, just a measly Pair of 8s. Not likely to win with three higher cards on the board and a possible Flush in Diamonds! Do yourself a favor: Practice dealing widows and figuring the best possible hands (High and/or Low). That way, unlike your opponents, you'll avoid common errors when playing with greenbacks!

Strategy: The starting hands with the best possible options include high Pairs (10 or above), one or two same-suited cards, and/or multiple consecutive cards. For instance, A♣ A♥ Q♣ J♣ is a nice one. And even though K♠ Q♦ J♦ 10♠ has no Pairs, its two high Flush draws and six possible Straight draws make it strong. The weakest hands have more than two suits represented, spread out denominations, no Pairs— or worse yet, Three of a Kind. Think about it—if you can use only two from your hand, that third card only hurts your chances to triple or quad up with the field!

Options & Variations:

- Instead of four, Tahoe deals three to the hand, no more than two of which can be used.
- In Oklahoma (a.k.a. Irish Hold 'Em) players are dealt four, but have to discard two of them after the Flop.

- Try keeping all four and splitting them into two two-card hands. Either at the end, figuring one hand for High and one for Low. Or at the beginning, optionally swapping cards between the two hands each round for a $2 fee (with no swapping after the River).

3-5-7

A multi-round, hand-shifting, gut-busting crowd pleaser.

"Nothing Beats a Great Set of Legs"

A "leg" is a chip used to keep track of a win or loss. It's a marker the player places in front of himself (not to be confused with the similarly placed stacks of chips used for fixed betting). Legs are especially handy in multi-round games (such as "3-5-7," just below) where players have to win a certain number of rounds before winning the pot. They may also be used in a negative sense, to mark the number of times a player passes or drops (as in "7/27" in Section 11 and also below in "3-5-7").

Playing: Ante. Deal each player three; 3s are wild.

Drop (a la Guts). Those who drop set a "bad leg" (25-cent chip marker) in front of themselves. If only one person stays in, that player sets a "good leg" ($1 chip marker) in front of himself. If more players stay in, the competitors compare hands, the winner gets a good leg, and the losers each pay the pot $2 (and get no leg). Deal every player (even those who dropped) two more cards. Now 5s are the only cards wild. Same drop, marker, and/or penalty procedures. Deal players two more cards. Now 7s are the only cards wild.* Same drop, marker, and/or penalty procedures.

From this point on, anyone with three bad legs is automatically folded. Reshuffle the cards and deal three to each player still in—3s are wild...

By the way, don't hold your breath for the ultimate sequence of hands (Three 3s, followed by two 5s, and then two 7s). It's almost six times more likely to see a fair coin come up heads 25 times in a row!

Forming the Hand: The rounds of 3 are Monte Carlo. The rounds of 5 and 7 are standard best-five.

The Reasoning Behind the Game: Dropping brings players closer to a forced fold, but minimizes a player's immediate risk. Although, in the round of 7, a player with two drops and lousy cards would have to decide between dropping (thereby folding) and staying in to pay the penalty. The mitigating factor of gaining knowledge would be absent, since the cards would be shuffled for the next round!

Winning: The first player with three good legs wins. A Flush is decent in the round of 3. Three of a Kind in the round of 5. And a Full House in the round of 7.

Example: I once got into a battle in which—looking back—I didn't have to invest a single chip. In the first two rounds I had great cards and quickly got two good legs. After that, instead of dropping and owing nothing, I got greedy, stayed in with a King-high and wound up having to hit the ATM. By focusing more on the money and the drama of the eventual showdown than my cards, I wound up losing more in that one hand than everyone else at the table the entire night!

Strategy: As a rule—especially in legs games—don't mistakenly think it's "your pot to win." Once the money's in the pot, it ain't yours anymore! So play tight and don't let your ego get in the way (like I did).

Options & Variations:
- Make the penalty pot-matching with a $10 limit.
- Three Plus Two (a.k.a. Three to Five) is 3-5-7's first two rounds, without the wilds.
- Two to Five—also no wilds—starts with Two-Card Guts and adds one card each round. Straights and Flushes count only with five cards.

Section 11 – Fundraisers

Attempts at quickly recouping losses.

Jacks or Better, Trips to Win (a.k.a. Jackpots)

Starts and finishes just as the name says.

Playing: Played as Five-Card Draw. But in order to open the first bet, a player must hold at least a Pair of Jacks. Starting to the dealer's left, players bet or pass (either because they can't or don't want to open). If no one opens, re-ante and re-deal the hand. After betting, exchange cards as usual. Bet and compare hands. The winner must have at least Three of a Kind. Otherwise, re-ante and re-deal the hand. If anyone folds, he's out for the duration.

The Reasoning Behind the Game: Using qualifying opening and winning hands not only leads to re-deals (which builds the pot), but also cuts down on players' ability to effectively bluff.

Winning: If you've got Trips (or better), play 'em!

Example: You're dealt 10♣ 10♦ 4♥ 2♣ A♠. If someone else opens, it might be worth calling. Ditch the 4 and 2, hold onto the Ace kicker and bet big. You're not going for a meaningless Two Pair. You're bluffing already having Three of a Kind—and crossing your fingers for a 10 in the last two cards!

Strategy: When at least one hand qualifies, more often than not, others do too. So you might not open with just Jacks, justifiably fearing another player has you beat. Another time not to open is when you actually have a decent hand (Two Pair or Trips already), but want to feel out everyone. (Raising an opener is likely to scare away other players.) In both cases, keep in mind that over a third of the dealings will have only one qualifying hand—meaning that you might be passing up a free shot at everyone's antes!

Options & Variations:

- Increase the opening requirements each re-dealt round to needing Queens, Kings, and Aces or better to open. (Still only Trips to win.)
- Jacks or Back plays that if no one can open, the hand is played out as "Lowball" (all-Low with a draw).

"The Over/Under"

Qualifiers can be used to determine who bets, if anyone wins, and the direction of the game. Sixty-Four combines all those factors. Deal it as Six-Card Stud, one down, four up, and one down. The player with the lowest hand showing leads the betting each round. It ends as High-Low with no declare. The High must have at least a Pair or it's all-Low. The Low must be at least a 9-down or it's all-High. If neither qualify, re-ante and re-deal the hand until one does. Sounds like a lot of qualifying—but I've never played it, just to qualify that remark.

Between the Sheets (a.k.a. Acey-Deucy, Red Dog)

A simple—but potentially costly—guessing game.

Playing: Ante $1. Deal two cards* face-up several inches apart (with enough room for a third card). Based on whether or not the player to the dealer's left believes the next card dealt (into the middle) will have a value between those of the first two, he either bids 25 cents or passes. If incorrect, the money goes into the pot. If correct, the player doesn't win anything, but keeps the 25 cents and earns a leg. Deal two new up cards onto the outer piles and rotate the guessing game clockwise. Players with one leg may bet up to half the pot—paying if they lose, but taking the amount risked from the pot if they win and earning a second leg. Players with two legs may risk up to the whole pot. But beware... If the middle card dealt matches either of the two outer cards, the player owes the pot double whatever he risked!

The Reasoning Behind the Game: To earn their first leg, players typically risk a minimum, since they can only lose that money.

Winning: When a player bets pot and wins, it's over.

Example: Your first two are a 10 and 4. You risk 25 cents, get an 8 and earn a leg. Later, the pot's up to $12.50, you've still got one leg and you decide to bet $6 on a Queen and 7. Another Queen comes up and you owe $12! Eventually, you get your second leg on a smaller bet. Finally, you're faced with a

If the first card is an Ace, the player declares it high or low before dealing the second card.

make-or-break decision: Betting on a 9 and 3, with $33 in the pot. A win puts you about $25 ahead for the hand. A loss...you don't want to think about that. Doubling up...you really don't want to think of that! But you have to. The smart play is to wait for a bigger spread. No need to be greedy and wind up the big loser for the night.

Strategy: Wait for spreads of five or more (i.e., a Jack and 5) before betting anything substantial. And make a mental note of what cards have been dealt. Faced with an 8 and 2, if you can't remember any other 8s or 2s having appeared, downsize your bet (for fear of matching up and owing double). Finally, set your sights on winning money, but not necessarily the whole pot. By taking little chunks at a time, you could come out comfortably ahead without risking your neck!

Options & Variations:

- Play with a $10 or $20 upper limit, instead of actually betting the pot.
- If everyone has money to burn, risk the money before seeing the two outer cards.

...With a Buy in the End

A last-ditch glimmer of hope...with a price tag.

Playing: After the final bet (but before the declare in High-Low), allow players to replace any one of their cards—50 cents for an up card or 75 cents for a down card.

Forming the Hand: It's standard to deal all replacement cards down. If it's to be an up card, it should be left down until everyone's done making their choices. The reason is you don't want to turn up a card and give away any information that might affect another player's purchasing decision.

The Reasoning Behind the Game: With fewer cards and betting rounds, Three- and Five-Card Stud tend to produce weaker hands and smaller pots. Adding a buy plays off players' optimism to build up both. The down cards are priced higher, based on the luxury of keeping their identities (and whether they've helped the hand) secret.

Example: In Three-Card, you're dealt [10♠] A♦ 2♠. A Flush is likely, but you don't want to get rid of the Ace. Replacing the 10 gives you a Pair draw, less-likely-but-stronger Straight draw, Low outs, and an air of mystery. Pay the 75 cents.

Strategy: Don't stay in with horrible hands just because you may get an extra shot in the end.

Options & Variations:
- It's often added to "Pass a Card, Buy a Card" (Section 2).
- Both Four-Card Three-Card (a.k.a. Gratz, named for a man who unintentionally misdealt Monte Carlo many years ago) and Six-Card Five-Card have an extra down card automatically built in. And both can still have a buy in the end.

7/27

If only there were a quicker way...

Playing: Ante. Deal each player one down, one up. Bet. Starting with the player to the dealer's left, players may take another card or pass. Mark each pass with a leg. When everyone's taken one or passed, bet and begin another round. Players with three legs can still bet, but can't take any more cards. When no one in a round takes another card, players bet and determine whose totals are closest to 7 and 27 without going over.

Forming the Hand: Aces are worth one or eleven, face cards are half a point, everything else is its face value.

The Reasoning Behind the Game: Factoring in the passing, the game can go into double-digit rounds, which translates into more betting and bigger pots for the winners!

Winning: Typically, the High hand is around 25 1/2. And the Low—if there is one—is about a 5. A hand of Ace-Ace-5 would win both ways.

Example: You're dealt [8♣] 5♥. Already over 7, you take a card...a pitiful 1/2-point King. The next rounds yield a Jack, another King, a Queen, and another 8. You're up to 23. You'll need more to win, but should pass. If you bet big enough (like you've made your hand), players may assume your down card's an Ace (which would give you a respectable 26). Pass and bet big in the next round and you may get a couple of players to fold. To end, take another card if you know another player's got you beat. Otherwise, pass and play out the bluff.

Strategy: With a starting total less than seven, pass and bet big enough to get any other players hoping to stay in going for twenty-seven. Above seven, take cards, but not blindly. Always keep track of face cards and Aces. It always comes down to those in the end.

Options & Variations:

- Instead of limiting the passes, go until no one takes a card (if you've got plenty of time to spare)!
- Allow over hands. In other words, a 7 1/2 would beat a 6. If two totals are equidistant from 7 or 27, either the lower one wins or the two split that part of the pot.

Blackjack (a.k.a. 21)

21 hits the home table.

Playing: Ante.* Deal one card face-up to each player (including the dealer), then another card (face-up for the players, face-down for the dealer). The player to the dealer's left is offered additional cards. If the player "hits" (wants some), he gets a face-up card and (if that card didn't "bust" him—put his total over twenty-one) may continue hitting until he busts or "stays" (doesn't want any more). Either way, the dealer offers the next player clockwise additional cards. When all the players have been offered a chance to improve their hands, the dealer turns up his second card. If the two total less than seventeen, the dealer deals additional cards face-up until the total is seventeen or greater. If in the process, the dealer busts, the dealer matches everyone's antes (which they also get back) who stayed in, no matter what their total. Otherwise, the dealer compares hands player by player and takes or matches their antes, depending if he wins or loses.

Forming the Hand: Aces are worth one or eleven, face cards are worth ten, everything else is face value.

The Reasoning Behind the Game: This sort of fast-paced, me vs. them game is the antithesis of home poker's purpose and should remain in the casino. I have a friend who likes the instant gratification of Blackjack at the end of the night. I'd mention his name, but I don't want to josh a wise man.

Winning: There's no typical winning hand. Nineteen, twenty, and twenty-one are solid hands you should always stay with, but even they can get beat or tied.

Since the dealer has to cover all the players' bets, this amount varies.

Example: You're dealt an Ace-7 (eight or eighteen). The dealer shows a 6. Since it's your first hit, several cards can help you and the dealer shows a bust card, you "double down" by placing matching chips next to your ante (which makes the dealer nervous). You automatically get one last card—a 2, giving you twenty. After the other players get their cards, the dealer turns over a 5. Now the players are nervous (because any ten could give the dealer an unbeatable twenty-one). The dealer hits...an Ace, for a total of twelve; hits again and gets a 7, for a final total of nineteen. You win!

Strategy: Although the object of the game seems to be players trying to get as close as they can to twenty-one, it's really about having as solid a hand as possible and hoping the dealer busts. Thus, players should always:

- Hit with a total less than nine
- Stay with any total greater than twelve if the dealer shows less than a 7
- Hit any total less than seventeen if the dealer shows at least a 7
- Double down with eleven
- Split Aces or 8s (Match your ante and separate the Pair. You'll automatically get a second card on each. Play them as two totally different hands.)

That's an extreme oversimplification, but should do you fine for these purposes. If you ever plan on playing for real in a casino, you'll want to more fully review what's called Basic Strategy before hitting the tables. There are rules for what to do in every situation with each total you can have against whatever up card the dealer shows.

Options & Variations:
- Instead of playing one hand for more money, play more hands for less. For instance, play two $2 hands instead of one for $5. This spreads out your risk and makes splitting and/or doubling down less expensive.

"When The Chips Are Down..."

Your once-impressive stacks are dwindling... Between hands, you can reach in your wallet, dig for dollars, and buy chips from another player. (If you do, set limits for yourself, such as no more than twice the original buy-in). In the middle of a hand, you have a couple of last-resort options:

1 *Play light*. Rather than putting chips into the pot, when betting, you counterintuitively take out chips. For instance, to bet $1, you'd slide a dollar's worth out of the pot. That dollar represents two dollars the pot is shy (the one you would've put in and the one you took out).

2 *Form a side pot*. Since you're essentially "all-in" and can't contribute any more, form a separate pot containing the other players' bets for the rest of the hand. Whatever happens, you lay no claim to that money.

Even with the below table to explain how to settle after implementing either option, it can quickly get confusing. Thus the least confusing option is not to play beyond your means.

You Play...	and Win	and Split	and Lose
Light	Take both pots.	Give the other winner the light chips, split the main pot.	If one winner, give them both pots—you still owe them another light pot's worth. If two, let them split the main pot, give the light chips to one—you still owe the other another light pot's worth.
With a Side Pot	Take the main pot, leave the rest for the next hand.	Give the other winner the side pot, split the main pot.	Others take/split both pots.

Section 12 - Vengeance & Triumph

Utter domination is the goal.

Illinois: (a.k.a. Black Mariah (2))

There will be no splitting.

Playing: Played like "Chicago" (Section 2), but the winner has to have both the best hand and high Spade in the hole! If the best hand doesn't have the high Spade or vice versa, re-ante and re-deal the hand.

The Reasoning Behind the Game: Greed. Whereas "Chicago" is one hand with a split pot, this is often multiple hands and one winner of a bigger pot.

Winning: The High hand varies, but is secondary to the high Spade—which tends to be the Ace.

Example: You're dealt [Q♠ 3♣] J♥ 10♦ K♠ 9♥. You've made a Straight and—since another player shows the A♠—have the nut high Spade in the hole! Since it's impossible to bluff (you can't win without a Spade), people should take the hint when you bet strong here on Sixth Street, unless someone has a Flush draw and wants the game to go on all night.

Strategy: Players without a Spade are tentative. So if you have one, bet strongly and hope others fold. It helps if you show scare cards (Two Pair, Trips, or four to a Straight or Flush).

Options & Variations:

• To win Royal Chicago (a.k.a. Two of Three), you need to have only any two of High hand, low Spade, or high Spade. Thus, being dealt an A♠ 2♠ in the hole is an automatic winner—an occurrence the average table of six or seven can expect to witness about one in every two hundred deals.

The Good, The Bad, & The Ugly

Get your hopes up, get your hopes down, get out.

Playing: Deal as regular Seven-Card Stud, except for the following: At the beginning, deal three cards face-down in the field (none of which will be common). After dealing Fourth Street up, flip the first field card. It indicates what's wild in players' hands. After Fifth Street, flip the second. Players must discard any from their hands that match it. After Sixth Street, flip the third. Players matching that card with any from their hand are immediately forced to fold. Bet as usual.

The Reasoning Behind the Game: Cruelty. A player could have a great hand (with a wild), then see it get pilfered and/or get killed.

Winning: A survivor should have Trips or better.

Example: At Fourth Street, you've got [10♦ Q♦] K♦ 4♣. "The Good"—the 4♠—made your 4 wild, giving you an open-ended Straight-Flush Draw. On Fifth Street, you're dealt the 8♦—giving you a regular Flush. You hold your breath as "The Bad" is flipped—whew, a 5! On Sixth Street, the Q♠ you're dealt doesn't really affect your hand. Then "The Ugly" is flipped…a 4. Muttering to yourself, you muck your cards and make a mental note of where the dealer parked his car…

Strategy: Bet in moderation until Sixth Street. Your whole world could change!

Options & Variations:

- When played as Five-Card Stud, fully deal out the hands before rolling each of the game's namesakes. (It makes for more betting and suspense.)
- Mexican Armpit is a "No Peeks" version. Flip all three cards at the start. The first indicates what the first player has to beat. The second what's wild. And players matching the third are deported from the game. So this version could be called "The Benchmark, The Good, & The Sender," but that really doesn't roll off the tongue.

Have a Heart

A goal for you. A plea from others.

Playing: Any player dealt a face-up Heart can immediately take any up card from any other player. The rest works just like regular Seven-Card Stud.

The Reasoning Behind the Game: Ruthlessness. A chance to better your hand at the expense of another. In a typical game with six or seven players, five or six Hearts will appear up.

Winning: Depending on the level of card swiping and counter-swiping, a player could finish with as many as eleven cards or as few as three. (Since Straights through Full Houses often win, a player with only three cards should fold in a heartbeat!)

Example: On Sixth Street you've got [10♣ 9♦] 2♦ 10♦ 9♥ 10♣ 4♥. (The 9♥ allowed you to steal the 10♣ from your neighbor.) And by way of the 4♥, you're about to get another. With no 10s in sight, you can't better your hand. But a player with a Pair of Jacks has been betting strong. Might as well hijack a Jack. At the very least, it helps your already-made Full Boat to be a little stronger (relatively speaking).

Strategy: In an early position, unless you're dealt Trips or a high Pair right away, fold. The players in the first two positions have the worst selection of cards to steal, should they get a Heart. And when other players get Hearts, their cards are always vulnerable. That adds up to players in an early position having a higher rate of...heart attack...heartbreak...heart failure... You get the point.

Options & Variations:
• Using any other suit is possible, but would wreck the pun built into the name.

Knock (a.k.a. Gin Poker)

Take what you need, knock when (you think) you lead.

Playing: Ante $1. Deal each player five cards. Place the deck in the center. The player to the dealer's left takes the top card from the deck and discards one from his hand face-up next to the deck. The next player to the left can either take the face-up card from the discard pile or one from the top of the deck, then discards one. Players continue to try to improve their poker hands. When a player feels he has the best hand, he knocks (and doesn't take a card). Every other player gets one last chance to improve his hand. Reveal the hands. If the player who knocked has the best hand, that player wins the pot. Otherwise, the failed knocker puts $2 in the pot, the player with the best hand does nothing and everyone else re-antes $1. Re-deal the cards and begin another session.

The Reasoning Behind the Game: Domination. Intimidation achieved through claimed superiority.

Winning: Depends on the session duration. A meager high Pair with a kicker could turn into a powerful Full House several rounds later...

Example: You're dealt Two Pair. Knock in the first round.* You may not win—or win as much—but if you futz around, it gives everyone else a better opportunity to improve. This strategy works best from an early position, so that not as many people will have two chances to better their hands. Not every hand improves every round, but you don't want to give that chance.

Strategy: If the game goes more than a few rounds without a knock, the discards will need to be shuffled. So be ambitious the first few rounds, knowing that the card you need might come back from the dead to help you!

Options & Variations:

• Rather than playing that a player has to knock to win, whoever reveals the strongest hand after the knock wins. But that yields smaller pots and doesn't encourage players to knock.

Unless one of the cards you need for the Full House magically appears in the discard pile!

Screw Your Neighbor
(a.k.a. Chase the Ace, Three Piles, King, Skinny D Takes Out the Trash)

Given the chance, they'd screw you.

Playing: Players set three piles—each totaling $2 in chips—in front of themselves. Deal each player a single card. Starting with the player to the dealer's left, each player may trade cards with his neighbor to his left. The neighbor must trade, unless he has the designated high card (either a King or Ace). The action continues to the dealer, who can trade with the top card on the deck. However, if the deck card is the established high card, the dealer is blocked from it and must keep the card passed to him! Players reveal their cards and the player with the lowest has to push one of his piles into the pot. Muck that round's cards and deal another round. When a full hand can't be dealt, shuffle them all and re-deal.

Forming the Hand: As alluded to above, either the Ace is high and 2 is low or the King is high and Ace is low. Clearly establish this before the game starts!

The Reasoning Behind the Game: Betrayal. A chance to project the anger you feel in being dealt an inferior card toward the undeserving player next to you, when in fact it's the dealer with whom you really have the issue. That's what a psychologist might say.

Winning: The last one left with any piles wins the pot.

Example: The player to your right trades you his lousy 4 ... and winds up with your lousier 2. Since you obviously now don't have the lowest card, just keep the 4. (Other players should confirm that they do not have a 2, rather than blindly assuming that they are safe and standing pat!)

Strategy: A 6 might be a safe card—or the death of one of your piles. In the spirit of not losing, keep track of what cards have been used and weigh that against how many people are playing. If you don't have a photographic memory, at least track the lows (2 through 5) and highs (Jack through Ace).

Options & Variations:
- Allow the dealer to accept the high card from the deck, but rotate the deal to be fair.
- Add a fourth, bigger pile behind the first three.
- Make the loser of the first round sweep the cards for the rest of the game and the loser of the second round fetch everyone refreshments for the rest of the evening!
- Play with an ante, legs, and matching instead of stacks. The lowest card each round has to match (half) the pot. The highest card gets a leg and a player wins the pot after earning a certain number of legs.

Additional Guts Games & Rules

With a drop, a chip, or a verbal declaration, Guts is simply a way of determining who wants to advance to the next round. But it's not always so simple...

When Everyone Drops
- **The Weenie** (a.k.a. **Wimp, Nelly**) **Rule**. Fine the player with the best hand $2.
- **Hold Your Guts**. Replay the same hand until someone stays in.
- **Progressive Guts**. Deal each player another card until someone stays in.
- **Pass Your Guts**. Pass a predetermined number of cards in a certain direction. Repeat and/or vary...until someone stays in.

For Those Who Stay In

- **(Blind) Auction Guts**. Deal an extra hand face-down. Before either the drop or the showdown, players bid for the right to switch their hand for the deck hand.
- **Beat the Deck** (a.k.a. **Ghost, Phantom, Dummy, Whiskey, Kitty**). Deal an extra hand face-down. In order to win, players must beat the deck hand. Sometimes—especially in draw games—the deck hand is given more cards than the players or more deck hands are used.
- **Crowd Penalty**. If everyone stays in, fine the player with the worst hand $4.

Counterintuitive

- **Blind Guts**. The go/no go decision is made without looking at the cards.
- **Re-declaring**. If only one player holds on the drop, give players a chance to change their minds by immediately conducting a sequential verbal declare.
- **Forced Guts** (a.k.a. **Blood & Guts**). Deal one of each player's three cards face-up. The player with the high card showing has to play. If there's a tie, both have to play. The card can be part of the hand or just an indicator. In the **Pinch** version, players call "Pinch" before the card they want dealt up. In the **Big Balls** version, the player with the high card may either fold for half the normal losing penalty or play the hand blind. When using pot-matching, use these rules only until the pot reaches an agreed-upon level.
- **Capping the Winner**. Set a fixed limit on how much any one player can win at once. (It just prolongs the game.)

Other Games & Variations

- **Spit**. After a two-card drop, reveal a community card for players to use in making their best Straight Three-Card or Monte Carlo hand.
- **Bloody 7s**. After a two-card drop, deal players still in three up cards. Any 7s down are wild. Any 7s up kill the player's hand, but relieve them of having to pay the losing penalty. (See "Two to Five" in Section 10.)

- **Double Death** has a three-card drop, then a High-Low declare based on players using only two of their three in either direction. All losers—including those who tie—pay double the usual penalty.
- **Four-Card Variations**. Standard **Four-Card Guts** ranks the hands from worst to best as High Card, Pair, Two Pair, Three of a Kind, Four of a Kind. Some variations draw up to two, three, or all four. **Four-Card Three-Card** is best three (Monte Carlo or Straight Three-Card) out of four. **Four Plus Three** has a four-card drop, adds three cards to the hands of players staying in, and ends with a Seven-Card High-Low declare. Players going both ways may use different sets of five in each direction.

SECTION 13 - Create Your Own

Unruly rules to consider.

After seeing hundreds of ways to play poker, you might be surprised to know there were plenty of variants that didn't make the list! Below is just a smattering of features that some people play, but weren't discussed in the book (for reasons that may be obvious).

Best Flush
Best Middle
No Checking
No Fives of a Kind
Aces Are High Only
Progressive Betting
Combining Split Games
Paying for Drawn Cards
Second-Best Hand Wins
Removing the 2s thru 6s
If You Raise, You Can't Win
Paying Extra for "Good" Cards
A Fine Is Charged for Misdealing
The Two Best Hands Split the Pot
Integrating Bridge or Other Games
Player to the Winner's Right Splits the Pot
Using the Cards' Pips to Determine the Split
Allowing Consecutive Cards to Equal a Wild

Betting the Maximum Only if a Pair Is Showing

A Particular Up Card Designates a Type of Split/Wild

Ranking Four to a Straight or Flush Between a Pair and Two Pair

Any Chips That Miss the Pot and Hit the Floor Belong to the Host

A Wild Card Can't Change Suit (to Make a Flush or Straight-Flush)

Any Two Cards That Add to a Certain Number Count as One Wild Card

In the end, some calls are blatantly idiotic. ("Eight-Card Stud with a Hold 'Em widow; Hockey Sticks and Mustached Men are wild; 6s count as 9s, 4s as 6s; 10s don't count at all, unless a prime-numbered Diamond is showing; the High and Low hands match the pot and everyone else splits it—unless someone gets a Joker in the hole, in which case he's out.") As a rule, if it takes more than 20 seconds to describe, can't be summarized by "It's like...but with...and..." or more than one person doesn't get it after hearing it described, it's not ready for prime time. Also be on the lookout for players who claim: "It's a little tricky at first, but you'll get the hang of it as we go."

Post-Play

After a session, take a few moments to process the answers to these questions:

- How well did things go tonight?
- What was out of my control?
- What could I have done better?
- Are there any positive/negative habits I hadn't noticed before?
- Did any particular games treat me better/worse than others?

Learning from experience is one way to become a better player. Another is by reading a healthy variety of highly focused poker books. Here are some of the classics, written by the giants of the game:

Thursday Night Poker by Peter O. Steiner, Random House, January 1996.

The Theory of Poker by David Sklansky, Two Plus Two Publishing, July 1999.

Caro's Book of Poker Tells by Mike Caro, Simon & Schuster, March 2003.

Scarne's Guide to Modern Poker by John Scarne, Fireside, September 1984.

Doyle Brunson's Super System by Doyle Brunson, Cardoza Publishing, 1979.

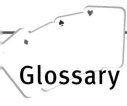

Glossary

Poker's filled with colorful colloquialisms. To supplement the many used throughout the book, here are some extras to help bolster your vocabulary. Just don't overdo it!

Cards

"Blank," "Rag" A (community) card that doesn't seem to help anyone

"Brick" A high card that "counterfeits" (ruins) a player's Low

"Bug" A Joker used as an Ace or to fill a Straight or Flush

"Buried," "In the Hole" Face-down

"Bullets" Aces—a "wired Pair" (in the hole) being "Pocket Rockets"

"The Case [Card]" The fourth of a certain rank

"Connectors," "Touching" Consecutive cards

"Cowboys" Kings; the "suicide" variety are of Hearts and Diamonds

"Door Card" Each player's first up card in Stud

"Deuces," "Ducks" 2s

"Free Card," "Free Ride" When everyone checks

"Hockey Sticks" 7s; also known as "Micks," in honor of baseball legend Mickey Mantle's uniform number

"Jakes," "Johnny's," or "[Fish] Hooks" Jacks; the "one-eyed" variety are of Hearts and Spades

"Ladies" or "Dames" Queens

"Kicker" The highest unpaired card in a player's hand; generally an Ace or King hoping to be paired up

"Off-Suit" Not of the same suit; multiple such cards form a "rainbow"

"Out" Helps a back-up plan

"Puppy Paws" Clubs

"Quatros" 4s

"Scare Card" Makes a strong hand look likely

"Snowmen" 8s

"Treys" 3s

Game Play

"[Numbered] Street" The card or round number (e.g., the door card in Seven-Card Stud is "Third Street")

"[It's Your Turn] to Act" To bid, bet, choose a card, or make some play/decision

"Advertise" or "Represent" Show certain cards to imply a particular hand

"Ante" A forced bet prerequisite to starting the hand

"Back Into" Unintentionally make a good hand

"Bad Beat" Frustrating loss; how a powerful hand is "cracked"

"Board," "Field," "Table Cards," or **"Widow"** Collection of common cards, often in a prescribed formation

"Bump" Raise

"Burn," "Bury," or **"Duck"** To purposefully waste a card by dealing it out of play, therefore making it "dead"

"Check-Raise," "Sandbag" To raise the bet after checking earlier in the same betting round; sometimes not allowed in home games

"Check to the Raiser" By not betting, not allowing a player who raised in the last round to do it again

"Clean/Wash the Deck" Thoroughly shuffle before dealing the next game

"Draw Out" To get a much-needed card that makes a winning hand "hit"

"Heads-Up" Two-players facing off

"Keep Someone Honest" Call someone's bluff

"Limp" To merely ("flat") call, rather than raising

"Loose" Taking too many chances

"Lock," "Doorknob" Guaranteed to win (at least half the pot, in a split game such as High-Low)

"Muck" To turn cards not in use face-down and put them into the pot or in front of the dealer

"The Nuts" Something unbeatable (i.e., an Ace-high Flush is the "nut Flush")

"The Pot Is Right" Everyone's put in the proper amount, versus when it's "light" and a player still owes

"Quarter the Pot" Divide the pot into fourths, usually after a tie in a split game

"Scooping," "Sweeping," "Swinging," "Hogging," or **"Pigging"** Attempting to win both ways in a split game

"Semi-Bluff" Strong bet when a winning hand could be made (as opposed to a regular bluff, when it couldn't)

"Showdown" or **"Reveal"** Determining the winner at the end of a hand; also the process of flipping one card at a time (i.e., in games such as "Anaconda")

"Slowplay" To weakly bet a strong hand, using "smooth calls" rather than raises, to keep players in

Hands

"An Art Gallery" Full of face cards (a.k.a. "picture cards" or "paint")

"Bellybuster," "Gutshot," or **"Inside" Straight draw** Cards missing in the middle of the sequence

"A Busted Hand," "Schmaltz," "Nothing," or **"Garbage"** A hand with no pair, usually a failed attempt at a Straight or Flush

"Chasing" Going after a hand not likely to be made

"[To Draw] Dead" A hand that can't possibly win

"A [Full] Boat" A Full House

"Natural" A made hand without any wild cards

"Open-Ender," "Outside" Straight draw Four consecutive cards to a Straight

"Pat" Made right off the deal; not requiring a draw

"Quads" Four of a Kind

"Rolled Up" Three of a Kind on the first three cards in Seven-Card Stud

"Smooth" The best possible Low with a given card (a "smooth 7" would be 7-4-3-2-1)

"Triplets," "Trips," or **"A Set"** Three of a Kind.

"Wheel," "Bicycle," "Baby," or **"Small Straight"** A 5-high Straight; a "Steel Wheel" being the Straight-Flush version

General

"Backdoor" Luckily "catching" the right card at the last possible opportunity, especially as an underdog; two in a row would be "runner-runner"

"Buy-In" The initial cost of chips required to join a game

"Calling Station" A "loose" player who calls too many bets; opposite of a "rabbit," who easily folds

"Cap" Limit

"Drop" To fold or "get out;" also, to lose money; or what a casino charges players to play there

"Fish," "Pigeons," "Geese," or **"Sheep"** Novice and/or poor players

"Hand" The current cards a player holds; or current game being played

"Open" The first to bet in a round (to "open"); also refers to cards showing (an "open Pair")

"Position" Strategically crucial seat at the table in relation to the dealer

"Pot Odds" The ratio between the amount of the bet to call and the money that could be won; especially important in contrast to the odds of making a desired hand

"Read" To get an impression of a player's cards by paying attention to their habits, actions, and reactions over time

"Rock" A passive, conservative player who doesn't enter into many pots; a more aggressive player would be labeled "tight"

"Round" A series of bets in a game; or series of games dealt by everyone at the table

"Shorthanded" Playing with not enough players (five is the usual home quorum)

"Steal" Attempt to get the pot when everyone else appears weak

"Tilt" Loose play based on frustration

"Up" A face-up card; an abbreviation for Two Pair ("Queens Up" is a Pair of Queens and an underpair); or to be winning that session ("I'm up $10 so far.")

Index